For two decades James Walter has watched as slavish compliance with Anglo-American political fashions determined Australia's shrinking future. The author and co-author of a number of studies of Australian political culture, including *The Ministers' Minders* (1986) and *Changing Cities* (1995), in this book James Walter has set out to describe, warn and offer an alternative.

Tunnel Vision

The failure of political imagination

James Walter

ALLEN & UNWIN

HC
605
.W459
1996

First published in 1996 by
Allen & Unwin Pty Ltd
9 Atchison Street, St Leonards, NSW 2065 Australia
Phone: (61 2) 9901 4088
Fax: (61 2) 9906 2218
E-mail: 100252.103@compuserve.com

National Library of Australia
Cataloguing-in-Publication entry:

Walter, James, 1949– .
Tunnel Vision.

Bibliography.
Includes index.
ISBN 1 86373 745 6.

1. Political parties—Australia—History. 2. Political parties—
Australia—Public opinion. 3. Australia—Politics and
government—1965– . 4. Australia—Economic policy—1965– .
I. Title.

324.294

Set in 10.5/12.5 pt Palatino by DOCUPRO, Sydney
Printed by Australian Print Group, Maryborough, Victoria

10 9 8 7 6 5 4 3 2 1

CONTENTS

INTRODUCTION

A defence of politics

A recent cartoon by Peter Nicholson directly captures the problem with which I am concerned in this book.[1] In one frame, captioned 1969, a young couple watches the moon landing on TV, saying, 'There's nothing we can't do'. The second frame, tagged 1994, shows the middle-aged couple, anxiously watching some current world disaster, saying, 'There's nothing we can do'. We all know this transition: people feel powerless, and they have given up on politics. And this includes people who, thirty years ago, dreamed of a new world, and from whose ranks many of our present leaders are drawn.

If Nicholson distils a widely shared impression, Hugh Mackay gives us the descriptive details: cynicism is so high that the nature of political institutions may have to be redefined; anxiety accompanies a feeling in the community that the two party system has lost its way or lost its point; traditional voting patterns have been destabilised; there has been a retreat from commitment; with the blurring of policy distinctions has come increased emphasis on the personal style of party leaders; leaders themselves rarely suggest that there are philosophies or policies which are distinctive to their own parties—it's an age of management and pragmatism.[2] 'All of this', says Mackay, 'has been watched by the electorate with a jaundiced eye. Personality politics may be fun, but there is a growing sense in the Australian community that there should be more to politics than this'.[3]

For all that, what is it that ties us together, all across the country, if not politics? We might be irritated by it and wish (like Malcolm Fraser did) to take it off the front page; but only the theatre of national politics gives a thread to our collective life. Sporting achievements can't provide the same coherence—there are too many codes, the metaphors of success are only momentarily compelling (at the height of 'the games'), thus there is no continuity—and nothing else comes close. When, as Mackay and others tell us is the case, there is widespread disillusionment and a call for national direction which politics can't provide, it's time to be seriously worried.

Have you given up on politics? Personally, I came closest to despairing of politics in 1991. In Australia we had a government that had achieved considerable economic reform, but that had reached the boundaries of what economically oriented policies could provide. And it had no new answers. Then, there was an opposition whose response to current problems rested on an even more 'rigorous' economism, whose only counter to the evidence of dissatisfaction was that we had to 'do it harder'. From London, where I was then working, it appeared even more dispiriting: the Australian opposition seemed incapable of registering the devastating impact that policies of the sort it proposed had wrought on the British social fabric.

But then there was a glimmer of hope: the political climate seemed to be changing. There was the Clinton presidential campaign in America, which appeared to revive the rhetoric of social concern. The British conservatives threw out 'the iron lady' and began to flirt with Keynesianism. And in Australia, starting with One Nation, the Labor government began tentatively to experiment with a new script. A surge of new books appeared which explored the 1980s, criticised the dominance of economic rationalism, and attempted to revive alternative policy approaches.

Was this the start of a new cycle, a cycle in which politics would more accurately relate to popular concerns? Would the scepticism and disquiet of most people be allayed, and some faith in the purposes of politics, and of the collective life, be restored? Well, yes—and no. Yes, in the sense that political leaders registered some of the limits of the ideas that had dominated the 1980s, and began to seek a new language of social concern. But no, in the sense that none of them seemed capable of delivering on their promises to produce programs appropriate to the new climate. In Britain, the conservatives lost any direction at all, and staggered from one crisis to another, appearing politically neutered and morally bankrupt. In America, the Clinton administration fought and won some notable battles, but was dogged by recurrent misjudgment, and shonky personal morality—the goodwill that might have sustained change dissipated. Whatever hopes Clinton inspired seemed lost in the rout of his Democratic Party in the congressional elections of 1994. In Australia, Keating called for a 'caring society' but was vague when it came to visions of what this might look like. His failure contributed to electoral defeat in 1996. The opposition, having abandoned one blueprint, seemed incapable of coming up with another. The conservative Coalition took power in 1996 with a promise of restoring 'comfort', and a piecemeal agenda. Political debate, just when it seemed on the verge of reviving, foundered. The best book on Australia in the 1980s, Paul Kelly's The End of Certainty, ended this way:

> The task of leadership now is to create a synthesis between the free market rationalism needed for a stronger economy and the social democracy which inspired the original Australian Settlement ideals of justice and egalitarianism.[4]

Yes, indeed! But nothing in Kelly's book suggests the grounds for such a synthesis, and many of the developments he lauds (as discussed in chapter 3 below) appear inimical to justice and egalitarianism, as I will show. Other books and articles that offered dispute and debate did not get the attention they deserved: it was as if the context in which they might be sensibly discussed didn't exist (see chapter 6). And as the improved economic outlook of 1993–94 appeared less sure in 1995, those whom Keating dubbed 'the Deficit Daleks' insisted (again) that a tougher economic strategy was the only solution. The things that had been taken for granted in the 1980s had run into the ground, but now we'd simply stalled.

Usually new leaders are produced by a new climate: they are people who express a message appropriate to, and definitive of, the new times.[5] (Bob Menzies, for example, remade himself as just such a leader in Australia in the 1940s). In the early 1990s, however, while the harbingers of change were evident, the voice of the future was strangled. In the past, new phases were accompanied by a kindling of the imagination, a new rhetoric of mobilisation, but now, it seemed, there was a general failure of the political imagination. What had gone wrong? Was there something about our times that had undermined politics, and had left us unable to respond to change? These are the questions driving this book.

But politics, you might say, is still all around us. We see it everywhere—the ubiquity of the leaders, the preoccupation of the media with political gossip, the factional battles in the parties, the obsessions with power. What, then, can I mean by politics having been undermined?

It is important not to confuse politics with power, or with government, or with doctrines. It involves all of these, but it is apart from (and prior to) them. It is, as Bernard Crick demonstrated thirty years ago in his small classic, *In Defence of Politics*,[6] an activity through which an aggregate of many members, with diverse ends, deals with the problem of self government. This activity involves negotiation, conciliation and compromise between different interests, and even different truths, as a means of reaching a workable solution to the problem of common rule. Crick traces the core argument back to Aristotle's assertion that 'a *polis* which goes on and on, and becomes more and more of a unit, will eventually cease to be a *polis* at all. A *polis* is by nature some sort of aggregation'.[7] There are other solutions to the problem of order—such as tyranny, kingship, dictatorship, despotism and oligarchy—which insist on a single interest, and so avoid politics. Politics, in accepting the simultaneous existence of different groups, recognises that no finality is implied in any act of conciliation or compromise: the door is always open. Hence, a healthy *polis* depends upon continuing political activity.

Politics should not be conflated with government—indeed, many governments insist upon a unity of interest to such an extent that they would suppress politics. Nor should politics be confused with power: struggles for power are struggles for power, and the unchallenged dominance of any one power will also impose a unity that is adverse to the *polis*. Political doctrines are attempts to conciliate diverse interests. But they, too, will be compromised: politics 'is not simply the grasping for an ideal, for then the ideals of others may be threatened; but it is not pure self-interest either, simply because the more realistically one construes self-interest, the more one is involved in relationships with others . . . '[8] Politics is not a system (like, say, Marxism), but rather a process. It does not lead to clarity, neatness or ultimate outcomes: the world is and will remain a hybrid and conflictual place. Order and secure communities can only be attained and sustained through the mediation which is the purpose of politics.

It is this sort of politics, arising from and recognising the problem of diversity, that I believe to have been undermined in the past twenty years. The pluralist *polis*, described by Crick (and Aristotle) depends on a balance between tolerance of diversity and conciliation driven by the community's interest in sheer survival. Politics is the activity that strives for the balance. But such pluralism is always in danger of overbalancing one way into monism (the belief that there is one fundamental solution to all of our difficulties) or the other way into radical relativism. Either is destructive of the *polis*. Both tendencies can be checked so long as we remain clearsighted about the importance of politics. Yet, as we have experienced increasing dislocation of the community in the face of globalising economic pressures, there has been resort to a single principle in public life, which we've been persuaded to call economic rationalism. This has undermined genuine debate—the diversity on which politics depends. Not only have we overbalanced into economic monism on one hand, but also there has been a radical relativism (deemed post modernism) at the heart of our intellectual life. We have therefore been denied the intellectual resources to 'speak the truth to power', as Edward Said has pointed out.[9]

A politics of diversity depends on there being something to negotiate about: doctrines have their limitations, but they summarise an idea of 'the imagined community'[10] to which they are addressed, and they contain a vision of a future to achieve. They are the essence of political debate, spelling out our options. When debate is superseded by monistic conviction we are told there are no options. This is in effect a veto on politics—at least the sort of politics I am talking of here.

Such a veto on politics lies behind the malaise of the 1980s, but now, as the climate changes, we discover that it has also deprived us of the tools to revive politics in the 1990s. This is the problem we must address if cynicism is to be overcome and hope in the future is to be restored. There is cause for anger at much that was done in the name of the economy and of sound management in the 1980s, and you may detect the undertow of anger in this book. But if we look at what has happened in historical perspective, there are also (as I argue in the final chapters) grounds for hope. In the recent past we have been neither angry enough, nor hopeful enough, and without the goad of one and the promise of the other, political imagination has been stifled.

We have not reached this point by accident, and much of this book describes how we arrived here. My framework can be simply explained. I believe that there have been three cycles in Australian public culture since the 1940s.[11] There is a common pattern for each: an accord, incorporating particular assumptions, is reached through political contest; that settlement dominates public life for a time, but eventually, usually due to changing external circumstances, it is seen no longer to 'work'; this then sets the stage for a battle over a new order, appropriate to the new times.

The first cycle (discussed in chapter 4 below) emerged from the post-war reconstruction battles, and—despite criticism and modification, especially in the 1960s—lasted until 1975. It was concerned with partnership between business and government, protectionist policies as the means to nation-building, and cultural assimilation. It failed in the end not only because of internal dysfunction, but also because it could not withstand the pressures of a globalising economic order.

The second cycle (explored in chapters 4 and 5) was inaugurated by the monetarist thrust of the Whitlam government's last budget in 1975. It saw the flowering of economic rationalism. Politics was driven off the agenda: there was no time for conciliation of diverse interests, no room for a contest of ideas. There was only one idea: that Australians must respond to the dictates of the international market. It was a time of prescription to, rather than dialogue with, the community.

Yet the benefits of the free market were illusory. Politics, devoid now of issues or principles, could only become a battle for power. Economic indicators improved, but most people found themselves little better off. Demands for a new sense of national direction, for accessible debate about issues, and for policies that would address social problems, emerged in the early 1990s.

By 1993, such demands were generating a third cycle, in which economic concerns began to be balanced by a call for a new politics of ideas. Prime Minister Keating, once an economic 'bovver boy', insisted that there was a need for a newly compassionate and caring society. In him, you could see the struggle to change, particularly evident in speeches calling for a politics of ideas,[12] and in his initial resistance to the resurgence of rigorously economic strategies in 1995. He did, after all, do as much as any figure in public life to exclude the sort of politics I am talking about from the public agenda during the 1980s (see chapter 5), and the necessary recovery involved remaking himself. He did not persuade the electorate.

For the conservative parties, the hurdles have been immense. Their obsession with 'dry' economics has put them a considerable distance from being able to address the needs that were revealed by Hugh Mackay's surveys. They have discarded the economic rationalist agenda contained in *Fightback!*, but, despite winning government, seem incapable of coming up with ideas that will shape the way this third cycle will develop. Until the brink of the 1996 federal election, they claimed to be keeping their powder dry, not offering hostages to fortune (or policies that Keating might steal!).

They won government by default. But if they fail to develop a new intellectual direction, one appropriate to the emerging political climate, they can only contribute to the disillusion and cynicism that constrains effective politics.

And what of the debate about ideas? The books criticising economics (Michael Pusey's *Economic Rationalism in Canberra*,[13] for instance), have been succeeded by books, such as Hugh Emy's *Remaking Australia*,[14] that argue a new economic agenda—not a return to 1950s protection, but a social market—at once communitarian *and* able to manoeuvre successfully within the international context (see chapter 6 below). If the constructive suggestions of these new books are not yet having the impact one might have expected, I suspect that it is because we have first to re-energise a politics capable of conceiving the general interest. The driving force may come from the emergence of genuinely popular movements for wholesale reform, and, as I argue in chapter 7, the debate about an Australian republic may provide our opportunity. If the need is for a new direction, a rethinking of what a heterogeneous nation can mean, the practical shape of new institutions capable of serving these ends will emerge from the disputes about a different sort of constitution. The cynics, the advocates of *Realpolitik*, will scoff, but they have forgotten what historians are now beginning to rediscover—that there was such a debate in the 1890s, that Federation cannot so easily be represented as a sellout to the bourgeoisie and the empire (the view Manning Clark did so much to perpetuate), but that it became a genuinely popular movement.[15] There are grounds for hoping that just such a debate can be generated again in the 1990s, but this time a debate directed to the needs and the voices of today's heterogeneous community. The success or failure of this debate will determine the tenor of this new cycle in the public culture.

Within this framework, each chapter has its own logic, but in an overarching argument. The first three chapters deal cumulatively with the premises of liberal internationalism— the argument that a better world is being created with the emergence of a free trading global economy in which Australia must find its place. The ideas behind this movement are overwhelmingly Anglo–American. Accordingly, the first chapter, Frontier stories, explores the results of the governing ideas of this 'new world order' in Britain and America, and the patterns of disruption arising in Eastern Europe where such ideas have been taken as inseparable from 'victory' over the discredited communist regimes. Australia, I suggest, has always been easily convinced that 'best practice' is to be found somewhere else, and has taken on the new ideology of best economic practice without sufficient regard for those signals that all is not well in the frontier states of the new world order.

Chapter 2, Transforming the Australian public culture, looks at the Australian interest in being included in the new international order through pursuit of 'the Asian objective'. This objective, shared by successive governments, is to wed the Australian economy to those of the Asian 'tigers' through ever closer trading and cultural links. We should not object to overcoming past myopia about the region and reaching better understandings with our neighbours, and the positive economic objectives are no more than commonsense. And yet, in exploring the way different governments reinvent 'Asia', and each claims to be 'discovering' it for the first time, we find that the character of current economic aspirations differs little from the mono-focal aspirations of the past (aspirations then aimed at integration into other great economies, such as those of Britain and America). While Asia is not a single entity, our political and economic rhetoric too often treats it as if it were. And Australia's 'Asianisation' provides a case study of the propensity of governments to allow a particular idea to drive all other options from the horizon. It is, too, a specific instance of the larger imperative, internationalisation, and its core ideology, economic rationalism.

Chapter 3, The message from 'the great Elsewhere'—the end of history?, deals with an emblematic text, Frances Fukuyama's, *The End of History and the Last Man*.[16] Already out of tune with the political climate emerging now, Fukuyama's book yet remains the best exposition of the beliefs which dominated the 1980s, and crystallised the *Zeitgeist* of the period in a way its adherents instantly 'recognised'. Revisiting this book helps us to understand both the power and the limits of the message which shaped public life everywhere. Parallel themes in the Australian context can be seen in Paul Kelly's, *The End of Certainty*,[17] which is also discussed in chapter 3. Both books, I suggest, are anachronistic, trying to impose on the past patterns and ideas that are only relevant in the present. We need histories more sensitive to the problems and options confronting earlier periods to understand their economics and politics. Such sensitivity might alert us not only to failures of vision, but also to sources of hope in those histories (an argument that arises again in chapter 7). But the crucial problems fudged by Fukuyama and Kelly are two: liberal internationalism does not in fact 'deliver' the universal economic wellbeing promised; and it comes to constitute a veto on local politics, crowding out alternatives and destroying political imagination.

The first of these problems is dealt with in chapter 4, Problems with the message. The dysfunctional outcomes of economic rationalism, on both national and international scales, and the damage to national political autonomy arising from liberal internationalism, have generated a substantial literature. It is nonetheless important to discuss some of the main elements of that literature, especially as they relate to Australia.

The second problem, which I describe in chapter 5 as the failure of political imagination, has not been sufficiently well understood. Here, therefore, I give extended attention to the way an authentic politics—a politics of negotiating diversity, recognising many ends, debating alternatives—withered in the face of the one big idea of the 1980s. This is the crux of the book (and the point from which I started[18]), and outlines the impasse which we must overcome if politics is to be defended, and the political imagination is to be revived.

Part of the project of revival is to insist that there *are* alternatives, and chapter 6, Constructive alternatives, reviews some of the alternatives that have been proposed. The argument here is that the synthesis between economic wellbeing and justice will be achieved only through a new defence of a mixed economy within the global market, and that there are strategies through which this can be sustained. And yet these constructive solutions do not seem to 'take' despite the changes evident in the political climate. This is, I suggest, because a politics of diversity and negotiation must be revived first, before alternatives can be admitted to the public agenda.

Thus, chapter 7, Reviving political imagination, reconsiders the very elements of a national politics. I start from the assertion that politics is about ideas, and not just about economics, or power, or management. (Economic rationalism itself is founded on an idea—of imagined social behaviour—rather than on a pragmatic grasp of the 'real' world.) Certain ideas—those concerned with citizenship, civil society and nation—will be integral to rethinking politics. Contemporary arguments about these ideas take us some of the way with the project of reviving politics. Reconsideration of the ways in which similar debates have been resolved in the past suggests that there is an ignored history of civic imagination and mobilisation from which we might learn. But, as I suggested earlier, it may be that we need to move from the abstract to the concrete, from ideas to the practical reform of political institutions entailed in constitutional change, to bring to the fore what we want our politics to be. The republican debate might be, as I suggest, one opportunity to initiate this project, but there will of course be no final answers. Politics, remember, always leaves the door open. It is the process itself we must defend.

CHAPTER 1

Frontier stories

What has been the most insistent message from our political leaders in the recent past? I think it was best summed up by former prime minister, Bob Hawke, in 1993: 'If the world decides it does not trust you, then it can ruin you'.[1] This sentiment is behind all the warnings which beset us when we raise concerns about local issues (can we, for instance, even think of public spending on welfare, or cities, without risking the judgment of irresponsibility—and retaliation—from 'the financial markets'?). Hawke's blunt conviction may startle, but it should not persuade us that his was an original insight. It is part of a continuous tradition. If you study Australian political rhetoric over time, you will find that there are three staple elements: that we are insufficiently aware of our own best interests; that those interests are always tied up with economic change elsewhere; and that we can only measure up by being alert to 'best practice' elsewhere.

Australia and the world

Our political elites have told us for a hundred years that we are a slumbrous, inward-looking nation, inattentive to the imperatives visited on us from abroad. Here is a familiar version of this message:

1

A major policy thrust of the Government has been to internationalise the Australian economy. By encouraging a more outward looking orientation, we are developing a more productive culture. This is essential if we are to adapt successfully to the challenges of a more rapid pace of change which improved communications and the globalisation of markets is forcing upon us.

Government actions . . . have . . . moved to adapt the economy to international competition and integrate it better into the world trading system. These actions are designed to focus previously protected industries' attention on world markets and international best practice . . . The effect has been to highlight all areas of the economy . . . where performance falls short of world standards. This new preoccupation with competition and efficiency is serving as a catalyst to change across the economy.[2]

Notice this statement's linking of economic efficiency with cultural productivity and its insistence on Australians being 'newly' outward-looking. In these essentials, it differs little from other—and much earlier—injunctions to the Australian people. The first prime minister, Edmund Barton, insisted on 1 January 1901 that the people be reminded of 'how rapidly and how radically the conditions of the world are changing', and that 'the wars of the future will be wars of trade'.[3] Sir Otto Niemeyer warned in 1930 that they must emerge from 'sheltered trades', and recognise that 'standards have been pushed too high' and must be adjusted 'to general world conditions and tendencies'.[4] Such a litany is a constant in national politics. Usually, good reasons can be given to support such views. But the recurrence of the strategy, and each generation's belief that its discovery of the need to look outwards is new, are curious. I think that this is over-determined, that it stems not just from the crises of the day, but from the deeper paradoxical impulse of what is still, after all, a settler society. Sylvia Lawson memorably captured the paradox this way:

Metropolis, the centre of language, of the dominant culture and its judgments, lies away in the great Elsewhere; but the tasks of living, communicating, teaching, acting out and changing the culture must be carried out . . . Here.[5]

Does our anxious focus on 'the great Elsewhere' undermine our ability to find our own solutions, and to fully realise a community, here? In part, that is what this book is about. But it also justifies starting from elsewhere. What does working and travelling in those countries to which we look for example suggest about the ideas we so earnestly seek to import into our own political life? How is 'best practice' manifest in the large market economies? What do the experiences of countries seeking to move from state-controlled to market-driven economies show?

From September 1990 to January 1993, when the ideas for this book were germinating, I was working in Britain, but travelled regularly in the rest of Europe (including Eastern Europe) and North America. Given the stress on market-driven change (in England and America) and on dismantling command economies to create 'free' markets (in Eastern Europe), I came to think of these places as frontiers of the new world order. I use anecdotes from that period at the frontier to open discussion on the nature of contemporary politics. These, then, are home thoughts from abroad.

The British disease

I'd lived and worked in London for a year or so in the early 1970s and remembered a city that was civil, well-served by public transport and culturally rich. For all the problems that were even then apparent, the welfare system provided the best sort of safety net—one that responded generously, positively and effectively to real crisis. Certainly there were other aspects of British society—under-resourced and unruly schools, racial tensions, a culture of secretiveness, the strong impress of class and hierarchy—but London seemed a city that worked and lasting impressions were positive.

Returning sixteen years later, in 1990, I found a city transformed. It wasn't just the disappearance of civility from the public domain, the ubiquity of beggars, the tent cities of homeless in Lincolns Inn Fields, the rubbish in the gutters, the pot holes in the roads. It was also the chaotic way in which the material aspects of urban life—'phones, water, gas, transport—were managed, by privatised bodies with limited accountability (despite their vaunted 'citizen's' charters), and no central coordination. This was a new frontier: a city in which commitment to the public weal had apparently been withdrawn. And it was a city that no longer worked well.

Just one instance was provided by public transport. It's an important indicator in any case—as a common resource facilitating exchange and communication, it underwrites community. And in a foreign context, where nothing can be taken for granted, you are reminded of how much our lives are shaped by the ways we move around our cities. In my view, you can tell a lot about a society by the modes of transport it fosters. Sixteen years before, London's buses and underground (tube) trains had provided efficient and comprehensive service. You could travel virtually anywhere speedily and relatively cheaply. By 1990, that easy mobility had been seriously eroded. Buses and taxis were terribly slow, impeded by the enormous proliferation of cars in the city. (The average speed of traffic in central London was 11 m.p.h. in 1990—when I left in 1993 it was between 6–10 m.p.h.) The underground trains had become very expensive. They were much more filthy, and forever being delayed by 'technical faults', 'passengers on the line' (or—euphemistically—'taken ill'), or security alerts. Did it have to be this way? Travel in cities as different as Paris and New York suggested otherwise. In Paris, the metro—once the poor cousin of London's tube—was cleaner, more modern, more reliable, equally comprehensive, and half the cost. (A British press report in 1992 showed the Paris metro superior to the tube in all these respects.[6]) In New York the subway trains had been cleaned up and modernised, a far cry from the squalid, rubbish strewn, graffiti embellished system I remembered from the 1970s. And a bus from Central Park down to the World Trade Center cost about the same as the cheapest bus fare in London (which would take you only a fraction of this distance) and half the cheapest tube fare.

How had the decline in London's public transport and the improvements in New York's and Paris's public transport

4

been achieved? In London, bus lines have been privatised, and though tube and rail services are still state subsidised, such has been the insistence since 1979 on 'market' returns on public 'investment', and users paying a greater proportion of 'real' costs, that rail and tube fares have increased enormously. Not surprisingly, there has been a fall in demand, as those who can afford to switch to cars. Hence with levels of 'income' incommensurate with sustaining the systems (which the government in turn has read as an expression of consumer preference—and a further inducement to reduce public investment), the rail and tube networks have been seriously under-financed for over a decade. The environment for public travel and the services have become much worse, while also becoming substantially more costly for the user. And the city's roads have become clogged with cars, making other ways of moving around the city frustrating, and inefficient. In Paris, there are also huge traffic problems, but at least policy seeks to address these. There, the philosophy is the obverse of that in London. Public transport is substantially subsidised—not because there is less commitment to market forces, but because there has been a different calculation about costs and benefits. It is reasoned that a city where people can get quickly and cheaply to their place of work, where their efficiency is not impaired by the frustrations of travel and their quality of life is enhanced by reduced pollution, where commercial exchange is not impeded by streets clogged with commuter traffic, will be an economically productive city. The costs of transport subsidies will be greatly outstripped by the city's gains in productivity. In Paris, therefore,

> subsidy is used as an explicit policy tool to encourage the use of public transport. Passengers meet about one third of the cost of travel, the rest is subsidised by the state and by explicit taxes on businesses in the Paris region. For the journey to work the subsidy is taken one stage further, with *employers* required to meet 50 per cent of their employees' travel costs.[7]

A similar reckoning is evident even in that quintessential market city, New York: there Metropolitan Transit Authority services are cross-subsidised by road users, via bridge and tunnel tolls, and from an explicit federal fuel tax which sub-sidises urban mass transit.[8]

For another fascinating insight into the changing British city, consider the fate of London's Canary Wharf development. The commercial regeneration of vast areas by private enter-prise was to provide the capstone of Thatcherism. Here, with London's abandoned nineteenth century waterfront, the larg-est port area in the world, was an intractable problem that no government had resolved since the war. Where the state had failed, private enterprise would step in, encouraged by the withdrawal of all forms of regulation in this 'enterprise zone'. In the zeal for reclaiming this 'abandoned' site, the community that lived there was marginalised. In the zeal for passing the problem over to the market, all forms of state provision to the new development (including transport provision) were ignored. In the belief that in the absence of state planning, commercial interests would make sensible strategic decisions, no one looked to the future at all. The developers appeared to give little thought to who would use the vast mono-devel-opments they generated; to how what they were providing balanced against what was already available in the city; or to how, even if people could be enticed to live and work there, they would travel to and fro. The docklands developments proved not commercially viable: it was hard later to see how anyone believed they could have been. And when those with the biggest interests in the project went broke, the British banks were so exposed that their only recourse was to make every bank customer pay the price in the form of increased interest rates on loans, overdrafts and mortgages. Far from the problem of city regeneration having been effectively solved, communities had been further disadvantaged, the national debt burden had been increased, and there are now acres of 'unusable' buildings that on current estimates will not be occupied in their lifetime, and that then, no one will be able to afford to demolish.[9] Is it better, in the end, to hand over large problems to private bureaucracies, accountable only to their shareholders, if the costs of bad decisions are still passed on to the community? How did we reach the point where it could be so readily assumed that public bureaucracies, accountable to the community through the political process for their decisions, were more likely to produce wrong or inefficient outcomes?

Cities and segmentation

In the media we daily find pictures of devastated cities representing economic dysfunction in the Third World, or in the former command economies which have not yet succeeded in establishing free markets, or in regions that have allowed ethnicity or religion to overwhelm secular politics. The messages are meant to be self-evident. But the devastated cities of the 'free' world are less often brought to our attention. Despite the deterioration in London I mention above, it is still the case that there and in the rest of Europe the debate about reclaiming the cities is a live one. In the United States, however, one is confronted with the realisation that some cities have been more or less abandoned—left as the repository of the most socioeconomically disadvantaged peoples, and allowed to rot. Bridgeport, Connecticut, is one such city.

Bridgeport was one of the major industrial cities of the north-eastern United States by the late nineteenth century, and a magnet for European immigrants. If it registered in my mind, it was as one of the great industrial successes of the American century. My visit there in early 1993 was inadvertent: I was staying with friends in a village outside Bridgeport, and needed to go 'downtown' to make travel arrangements. My friend offered to drive me, and to show me the city centre which, he assured me, was 'something to see'.

There is little left as a monument to past achievement; what he showed me instead was a ghastly theme-park of de-industrialisation. Bridgeport had not moved fast enough to new technologies and new industries, and had not been able to compete in the post-war scramble for international industrial advantage. Neither, you might argue, had cities like Liverpool or Glasgow, but there the fight to revitalise the city is still evident. Not so here.

Downtown was, in large part, boarded-up. No attempts to refocus the city economy had succeeded, the city centre had not been 'gentrified': the major firms had simply closed shop. It was startling to see a vast Sears Roebuck store abandoned, perhaps because movies have made department stores icons of the American way of life. Huge multi-level car parks were empty ('they're used only for drug deals or killings now—it's dangerous to park there,' said my friend). Occasionally pedestrians—all of them black—ambled across the streets. At one intersection, a decrepit car with no brakes drifted through a red light and when we stopped—just in time—the black driver simply gave us the high sign and drove on: 'there's one rule to observe down here,' said my friend, 'whites never have the right of way'. The residential streets around the city centre were still full of once substantial houses from the 1940s and 1950s, disconcertingly familiar from such myth-creating TV series as 'The Wonder Years', but now in extreme disrepair, though still clearly occupied.

We drove down to the waterfront, to grubby beaches, and the University of Bridgeport. 'This was a state college, started in the mid-forties,' said my friend. 'It used to have a reputation in things like engineering, but it looked like it would fail a few years back. For one thing, the dorms were too close to what had become virtually a ghetto: students kept getting mugged and raped and even shot on the way to class. Nobody knew what to do. Then someone in the city came up with a bright idea: they sold it to the Moonies! God knows how they'll make a profit from it.'

My friend, who worked in a neighbourhood resource centre for inner city kids (raising money to keep it afloat) explained that the real economy of the city was drugs. The Connecticut turnpike (built in 1958) sliced right through Bridgeport (incidentally, severing the waterfront and commercial centres from residential areas—which some saw as contributing to the city's decline). Easy interstate road access for dealers, with exits right into the most disadvantaged high unemployment areas, was thus achieved quite fortuitously. For fast transportation and distribution to a target population with high levels of alienation, frustration and boredom, the situation could not be bettered. 'The only people who stay here now are those who have no choice.'

The majority of the white population has left, to live in the pretty Connecticut villages outside town. The expensive homes of the children of all those hard-working immigrants are strung out through the 'woods', and one turns a corner on a heavily forested country road to come upon an expansive and well-maintained shopping mall.

Now, we all know that the big US cities—New York, Chicago, Los Angeles—present problems, and that the flood of the disadvantaged into these world cities has created counterposed ethnic enclaves. We also know that most Americans do not live there, and I guess we assume that there is another America where such problems are not so endemic. The visit to Bridgeport, however, showed nothing so clearly as the deep segmentation of the American population. Such are the contradictions produced by the American dream.

An Eastern frontier

My next story takes place in Budapest, summer 1992. The bus routes in Budapest are difficult to work out. The subway— though clean and new—gives limited coverage of the city. Tourists like us take to the taxis, which are plentiful. The cabs are mostly old, their decrepitude advanced by the high speeds at which they are driven over cobbles and other appalling road surfaces. Drivers have limited competence in languages other than Hungarian, and their meters are extremely variable: some turning over at breathtaking speed to generate a fare three or four times that you paid in another taxi over the same route. Complaints are greeted with incomprehension or menace. One pays.

One evening in high summer, a group of us—Australians in Budapest for a conference—are travelling by taxi to the conference dinner. In town for a couple of days now, having had time for sightseeing, we feel like we're coming to terms with this city. As the taxi careers through downtown, we swap horror stories of taxi scams experienced around the world.

We turn onto the Freedom Bridge, crossing the Danube towards the Gellert Hotel where the dinner is to take place. The hotel is an extravagance from the end of the Austro–Hungarian empire. The bridge is gently arched—from the middle, the crest, there are long outlooks on the city, the hills, and the grand hotel itself.

As we sweep down towards it, by now fully engaged in architectural critique, there is, suddenly, a loud explosion. The passenger in the front seat—a distinguished Australian poet—slumps, groans and clutches his face, muttering, 'My eyes! Christ, my eyes!'. We, in the back, feel a stinging sensation across our faces; someone cries out. There is a thin mist on the window next to me. Was something thrown into the cab (the window in front is open)? Was it a shot? Was anyone on the pavement just there—it didn't look like it, but looking back and at this speed, it's hard to tell.

The driver pushes his rattling cab even harder over the last few hundred yards, through an intersection and into the hotel car park, then brakes vigorously. We fall out of the cab, the poet still kneading his eyes. The driver wrenches open the car's boot, pulls out a jerry can, and starts to douse our friend's face with water. It's apparent now that, whatever the cause, some corrosive liquid has been sprayed through the taxi—and that he has copped most of it in the face.

Our alarm and anxiety is given a focus (I can already imagine the headlines, 'Australian poet blinded in terrorist attack', 'Tragedy at ill-judged conference in Eastern Europe'). Someone runs into the hotel for help. Another passenger finds the remains of a small cannister on the floor in the taxi. We show it to the driver. We can't understand a word he says, but his meaning is unmistakable—he knows nothing.

One of the hotel staff walks unhurriedly out to the car and talks to the driver, then turns to us, saying, 'It is painful now, but it will pass'. 'But what is it? Where did it come from?' we ask. He shrugs, and walks away. Our anxiety is turning to anger. The driver can see what is coming. He hurls the jerry can back into the car, leaps in and accelerates away into the traffic. (It was our only free ride in Budapest.) It's dawned on us now that it's probably mace, that the cannister was in the cab all along, and almost certainly belonged to the driver. It was just one of the proliferating anti-personnel devices of urban life. Rolling around the floor, agitated by the vibration of fast travel over rough roads and high summer temperatures, it had reached critical point and exploded.

Two questions now: should we get medical help? Should we call the police? Our friend is already coming around. Though his eyes remain alarmingly bloodshot and swollen, he can see again, and the pain is abating. He refuses medical help. As for the police, an Australian official—in the hotel for the dinner—advises us that there's no point calling them for a case like this. He tells us the story of an acquaintance who lives in a palatial house near the Australian Embassy in the Buda Hills, outside town. Someone had thrown a Molotov cocktail against this man's front door as a means of breaking in. He called the police immediately. Fortunately, the door and the house had withstood the firebomb (the party apparatchiks had known what they were doing when they originally built those villas). The police arrived twenty-four hours later. The lesson, the official says, is that effective policing disappeared with the downfall of the communist state. The service had been so implicated in the old regime that it was more or less abolished. But you can't build a new police force overnight. So there is only a skeletal service, too stretched to cope with anything but major catastrophe. People have to look after their own security. That's why taxi drivers carry mace.

Hungary has long been one of the more congenial, open and enterprising of the former Eastern bloc countries. Its problems are certainly less than those of the states of the former Russian confederation. Yet there is still considerable, and justified, anxiety there about the future—and if there, how much more further East? This anxiety seemed first to induce a belief that rolling back the power of the state, assuming as quickly as possible the practices of a 'free market', would provide solutions. This was exacerbated by the tub-thumping of the Western media, trumpeting 'we have won the war, we've defeated communism: what is there left to do?'

What will happen when the attempts to generate 'free markets' fail to meet the expectations of these newly 'liberated' populations? Untrammelled capitalism is an efficient way of stimulating enterprise, producing commodities and creating wealth. But it will not efficiently distribute wealth, provide employment for all, feed the hungry, house the homeless, ensure a reasonable quality of life, provide for environmental regulation—the list could go on—as (Western) liberal reformers since the 1870s have realised, and as a survey of attempts to 'deregulate' Western polities in the last decade demonstrates (need we go further than Thatcher's Britain or Keating's Australia?). Yet the tortuous struggles to balance the collective interest with the dynamics of the market place in non-communist countries—especially since the 1940s—are forgotten as we push the most open slather models of economic relations on the former communist regimes. The ideological impetus is clear—these are at the furthest extreme from the former state command economies. But we know these nostrums won't serve to provide a better life for all (though significant minorities will do very well). They will erode even further any sense of civic culture and public responsibility, and the welfare of the least well-off may be even more ghastly. So—turning a blind eye to 'the market'—we resort to bandaid solutions: selective food aid, loans, and the 'advice' of the IMF. This won't be enough to prevent the shift of opinion already evident in the resurgence of socialism in the Hungarian elections of 1994. Electoral swings suggest that the 'free market' is on notice in much of Eastern Europe.

It won't take widespread impoverishment (though this is more than a possibility) to generate huge disaffection, just the perception that expectations of a better life have not been met. Then think of the potential for rivalry and conflict in a context where the old civic cultures have been rendered illegitimate. Yugoslavia gives a chilling portent. Think of what the Balkans used to represent—before they were 'united' under the communist heel they were the site of bloody, prolonged internecine conflict. How many of the emergent Soviet states might manifest such tensions? What of Russia itself? Yeltsin's mobilisation of troops against parliament, and the subsequent election of a rabidly nationalist and counter-reformist populist leader, Zhirinovsky, in 1993; the maladroit, bloody response to the unilateral Chechen assertion of independence in 1994–95—these may be just harbingers of what is to come. And despite American attempts to negotiate the relinquishment of nuclear arms by some former Soviet states, remember too that the destructive weaponry of the Soviet state is still largely in place, yet in a real sense no one is in control. In the face of the potential for such disaster, bandaid solutions and neo-classical economic dogma simply won't serve: radical solutions and international cooperation on an unprecedented scale will be needed. Can this be achieved?

The economics of a better world?

One of the governing assumptions in recent public debate has been that we now know enough about the economic dynamics of social life to create a uniformly better world. Problems remain, to be sure—the former Eastern bloc countries have yet to achieve the transition to these new dynamics successfully, and much of Africa has a long way to go (though the 'tiger' economies of Asia show it can be done). But the fundamentals—deregulated markets and liberal democracy—are universally recognised. The collapse of the chief opposition to these ideas in the failure of communist regimes is argued to be a key indicator of the 'truth' of such tenets. In Australia, the idea that they're getting it right elsewhere resonates with a tradition of anxious attention to the larger world, and fuels such messages as that with which this chapter opens. We must (yet again) make sure of a secure place in that world by entering the game on the terms dictated by 'the great Elsewhere'.

The experiences I've recounted above are intended to raise questions about whether such assumptions should continue to be persuasive. Can we continue to believe in the message from the great Elsewhere? The assumptions at work in such leading Western economies as Britain and America, judging on their outcomes, are deeply flawed. Yet these are the very assumptions that are to be translated into societies in even deeper crisis, those of Eastern Europe, as their salvation.

In the face of the collapse of public order in Eastern Europe (the cowboy entrepreneurialism of Budapest taxi drivers, and the frontier ethos of self-protection there, are as nothing compared with what is happening in Russia), or confronted by the fact that Russian people tell us that life is 'harder and scarier'[10] there now than under communism (and they are attracted by ultra-nationalism and ethnic solutions), we insist that economic reform must be pushed even more vigorously—it is the only answer. The merest survey—take the Docklands Light Railway to Canary Wharf, visit Bridgeport—should provoke scepticism. What failure of imagination blinds us to the void between what is promised and what is achieved? Isn't there a gap between what is everywhere said (the economic solutions to the world's problems are in sight) and what we see around us (the devastated cities not only of the East but also of the West)? If so, how is the rhetoric of economic progress maintained, and what have been its effects on our politics?

CHAPTER 2

Transforming the Australian public culture: European myths and Asian realities in the 1980s and 1990s

If we are to look outwards to the world for best practice, where in particular are we to look in relation to our future? Our future depends, it is said, on successfully integrating with our region, and hence we have been especially urged to look to Asia.

A preoccupation in Australian public life in the past decade has been with how to marry geography with history. T B Millar distils the problem in an illuminating discussion of 'geography versus history'.[1] The question is: how can Australia, which has emerged over the past two hundred years as a predominantly white immigrant country whose peoples have brought with them a European heritage, find its appropriate place in the Asia–Pacific region in which it is located? Here's former prime minister, Bob Hawke:

> . . . one of the truly foundational issues of our national life . . . (is) our relationship with Asia. That issue has been with us . . . since our foundation . . . in 1788 . . . Since that time . . . we have been struggling to reconcile the facts of our geography with the preoccupations of race, of history and of sentiment.[2]

Elsewhere, then Foreign Minister, Gareth Evans elaborated:

> For most of the 200 years since European settlement, Australia has fought against the reality of its own geography. We have

15

thought of ourselves, and have been thought of by just about everyone else, as an Anglophonic, and Anglophilic outpost—tied by history, language, culture, economics and emotion to Europe and North America.[3]

The question, as Evans put it, is how can Australia, the 'odd man out', become the 'odd man in'?[4]

Governments and policy makers have recently been in no doubt of the answer: it is forcefully to effect a policy reorientation towards Asia, and to press for public education to promote 'Asia-literacy' within the Australian community. I do not question the need for Australia to put aside the racist elements in its past, or the need for it to be more attentive to the regional community in which it is located. I support doing everything possible to improve productive relations—including trading relations—with Asia. But by looking at the arguments that have been made in support of these objectives, I wish to raise the underlying assumptions for consideration. It is edifying to ask what these assumptions reveal about the 'imagined community'[5] being addressed by the policy makers. It is illuminating, too, to ask in what ways, precisely, do these assumptions differ from those voiced in earlier phases of Australian history? It is interesting, finally to ask: whose assumptions are these, who is voicing these messages?

The ALP government and the Asian objective

There was consistent stress on what we might call the 'Asian objective' throughout the term of the federal Australian Labor Party (ALP) government, elected in 1983. But there has been a considerable efflorescence in that objective over recent years.

The economic agenda was elaborated in Ross Garnaut's immensely influential report for the government, *Australia and the North-East Asian Ascendancy* (1989).[6] The Garnaut Report has been widely discussed elsewhere[7]—for my purposes here it is useful simply to recall its essentials:

Garnaut argues that the recent rapid and sustained period of growth, especially in Japan, Korea and Taiwan, has shifted the centre of gravity of the global economy away from Europe and North America to the Asia–Pacific region. Thus, Australia has to prepare itself to play a part in what many are now calling the coming 'Pacific Century'. Rather than seeing Northeast Asian growth as a threat, Garnaut suggests, we need to identify opportunities to be grasped: but this will only be possible if Australia quickly adopts a set of more appropriate policies. Central to the design of these policies must be the acceptance that Northeast Asian growth was dependent upon the export orientation of these economies: thus, Australia's response needs to be based on the dismantling of our own system of tariffs and other methods of protection, and we must use our voice in the international arena to persuade the rest of the world to do the same.

At the same time, these economic policies must be backed by major efforts in education and research to make Australia more aware of the languages, cultures and economies of Asia . . . We should not fear the continued success of Northeast Asia because there is a strong degree of complementarity between the economies of Australia and Northeast Asia.[8]

Hard on the heels of the Garnaut Report, and complementary to it, was the Foreign Minister, Gareth Evans, statement on *Australia's Regional Security*, tabled in parliament in December, 1989. Evans identified the essence of his statement as:

. . . the theme that the policy responses . . . available to protect Australia's security are multi-dimensional. They go well beyond strictly military capabilities . . . They also embrace traditional diplomacy, politico-military capabilities (in the border zone between defence and diplomacy) economic and trade relations, and they extend to immigration, education and training, cultural relations, (and) information activities . . . all should be regarded as mutually reinforcing contributions to our security.[9]

This multidimensional approach to policy has influenced Australia's commitment to a non-discriminatory immigration policy, the removal of protectionist barriers and deregulation of the economy to make it more open to the economies of the region, a new defence self-reliance no longer founded on drawing 'great and powerful friends' into the region, and constructive foreign/economic policy initiatives such as the

Asia–Pacific Economic Co-operation (APEC) process and the Cambodian UN Peace Plan.[10]

The APEC forum was the keystone of the Labor government's Asian initiatives. First mooted by Bob Hawke in 1989, and developed through annual ministerial meetings of some eighteen Asian–Pacific countries, including the United States of America (USA), between 1989 and 1993—when it was elevated to a meeting of country leaders at Paul Keating's suggestion—it has become the major forum for regional economic thinking. It is unlikely that the Coalition government elected in 1996 will resile from this initiative. An Australian initiative, and one given momentum by the vigorous commitments of both Hawke and Keating, it has been described as Australia's greatest international contribution since the war. Australian leaders have stressed that APEC is about building community, achieving regional cooperation, and linking nations in ways that will drive economic development and sustain security. Most APEC documents stress trade liberalisation above all else: what social vision the forum encompasses is subsumed under such headings as 'human resource development'. An important consideration has been the effect of the forum in countering the isolationist tendencies of the US, and keeping it economically committed to the region. For Australia's purposes, APEC has been the means of working towards achieving the agenda described in Garnaut's 1989 report. But it was also an important strategic tool, not only in foreign but also in domestic politics, for Paul Keating. As Greg Sheridan observed:

> For the Prime Minister, Mr Keating, . . . (APEC) is the magic pudding. It solves all strategic, economic and even cultural problems. It is the means to keep the United States constructively tied to East Asia; it is the means to moderate US–Japan tension; it is a way to handle the emerging power of China; it is a highway for Australia to drive down towards the region; it is a provider of strategic spin-off benefits as the 18 Asia–Pacific powers meet regularly, develop a collegial spirit, solve problems in advance. It is also becoming the chief rubric of economic and even cultural links between Australia and her northern neighbours. It is the site of statesmanship, the vessel of leadership, the chalice of history.[11]

APEC was, thus, a focus of Keating's leadership claims, but also a reference point in his energetic attempts to transform the domestic culture. He spoke enthusiastically of a national culture shaped by, and helping to shape, the cultures around us.

Along with the outwardly oriented effort to raise and improve Australia's profile in Asia, there has been a strong prescriptive approach to domestic policy: our business people and entrepreneurs must develop existing links, establish new links and learn to live with economic reform; we must broaden our efforts through schools and universities to educate more people about the values and cultures of societies in our neighbourhood.[12]

All of this implies that Australia stands opposed to a relatively unified, undifferentiated region: indeed the metaphor of Australia as 'odd man out' depends on this implication being accepted.[13] Further, this series of policy pronouncements depends for its persuasiveness on the idea that Australia has been too Eurocentric for too long: 'an Anglophonic and Anglophilic outpost'. Australians have thus known nothing about Asia—they have remained self-satisfied and ignorant.[14] This has been in some sense to ignore reality: 'no country or group of countries can any longer stand outside the mainstream flow'.[15] But why is this only being recognised now? Essentially, because as a society, it is said, we have grown and evolved:

> We are not seeking the same sort of acceptance now that we sought as an isolated, settler nation of moderate importance in the international scheme . . . through our special relations with the British, then with the Americans. We are now . . . following a more mature path.[16]

That said, however, the key imperatives are economy and security, with complementary, interdependent economies tying into common, collective security. Thus, on the one hand:

> . . . the greatest problem facing Australia is the persistent deficit in our current account . . . There is no solution to that problem which does not involve Australians selling more to the countries of Asia . . . [17]

19

And on the other:

> The central idea of 'common security' is that lasting security
> . . . (lies) in a commitment to joint survival, to taking into
> account the legitimate security anxieties of others, to building
> step-by-step military confidence between nations, to working
> to maximise the degree of inter-dependence between nations:
> putting it shortly, to achieving security *with* others, not *against*
> them.[18]

So what is new?

We can ask some questions about these assumptions. Does
Asia have common concerns which Australia has wilfully
ignored? Just how new is this concern with Asia: what part
has Asia played in the debate about Australian nationalism
and Australian consciousness? What is the nature of our Asian
ignorance? If there is now a 'mainstream' (interactive regionalism on a world scale?) just how has Australia been able to
stand aside from it for so long? Is it productive to talk about
relative levels of maturity in national life? And just how
distinctive are the current concerns with economy and security
when compared to the incentives behind Australia's foreign
relations in the past?

D A Low has addressed the 'fundamental misconception'
that lies behind the persistent metaphor of Australia as 'odd
man out'.[19] The notion that Australia's history makes it special—and anomalous in Asia—does not sufficiently take
account of the 'anomalies' that differentiate the other countries
of the region: the demographic disparities and population
admixtures that distinguish one from another, and above all
the extent to which many of them find their cultural roots not
within their own countries, but elsewhere—Singapore in the
traditional values of China, the Muslims of Malaysia and
Indonesia in the Middle-East (Mecca above all), the Buddhists
of Sri Lanka, Thailand and Burma in north India, the Hindus
of Bali in India, too, the elite Filipinos in Catholic Spain, and
so on.[20] To what extent, then, are Australia's cultural roots in
Europe so unusual? The fact is that the practice of regarding

Asia as homogeneous is a product of the European imagination, where the 'Oriental' stood for an undifferentiated 'other' marking off the bounds of what was thought to be special in European civilisation.[21] In that sense, it is part of the cultural baggage a migrant people carried with them to Australia.

To be fair, the former Australian foreign minister did sometimes—contradicting his Australia as 'odd man out' metaphor—concede the heterogeneity, diversity and even cultural conflict between the countries of the region.[22] Even so, he wanted to argue, Asian countries do have a common concern which sets them apart:

> If there is any single unifying element in the sprawling
> diversity of Asia, it is probably the pragmatic preoccupation
> with economic issues which now characterises almost every
> country in the region.[23]

Given the urgency of the pragmatic economic imperative in his own message, however, one might have thought Australia shared this preoccupation, and was central (rather than peripheral) in the economism driving foreign relations in the region. Economic concerns have certainly been to the fore in the APEC process in which Australia has been so important. Further, it might be said that historically one of the defining characteristics of a settler economy such as Australia's is the concern with economic advantage[24]—a point I return to in chapter 4.

Interest in the countries of our region was not an invention of the recent Labor government. It influenced the agenda of the Fraser Liberal–National Country Party (L–NCP) government (1975–1983), whose concerns were expressed in very similar terms to those we have seen above.[25] The Whitlam Australian Labor Party (ALP) government (1972–1975), moreover, made much of its attempts to pursue new relations with the countries of the region.[26] The present Coalition government has endorsed such sentiments. What is notable is the way in which all of these governments have built on a long history of discussion of Asia within Australia, while simultaneously claiming to have discovered the problematic nature of Australian relations with Asia anew.

21

Asia, at least in the sense of the European imagination of Asia, has always figured in Australian consciousness. John Docker has shown that the nationalist imagery of the nineteenth century was not as unified, monolithic and white racist as we now imagine it to be. Australia was then more cosmopolitan both in fact and in its concerns than it was to become after the First World War. In particular, a fascination with the 'Oriental' could be detected in popular culture.[27] Annette Hamilton has also provided an analysis of the way Asia figured as 'the other' in Australian consciousness.[28] This fascination was an incentive for some to seek to know about Asia, and books about Asia appeared relatively early on the national scene.[29] Walker and Ingleson detail the publication of some 'profoundly appreciative' responses to Japanese civilisation by prominent Australian men and women of letters—such as Douglas Sladen, James Smith and Rosa Praed—in the 1880s and 1890s, and of the enormous respect accorded Japan in books and newspaper articles by such as A G Hales and Colonel George Bell after the turn of the century.[30] This was not the only story, there was 'invasion fear' literature to match it, but Ingleson and Walker remind us that 'what can be . . . designated pro-Asian sentiment has been glossed over or forgotten so routinely that it can appear that the only available response to Asia was a hostile one'.[31]

Even after the First World War, the effect of which was to encourage Australia to become much more narrowly an empire-oriented white enclave,[32] there were important developments. The first tour of South-East Asia by a government trade envoy, John Latham, took place in 1934. The popular success of Frank Clune's *Sky High to Shanghai* (1938); the attempts by the Australian branches of the Institute of Pacific Relations (IPR) to promote 'patient, impartial, scientific investigation' of the region; the argument by Australian historian Stephen Roberts at the first IPR conference in 1925 that 'White Australia' hampered industrial growth, fostered higher wages and an uncompetitive labour market; the thorough demonstration by Jack Shepherd of the commercial potential of the region in his 1939 book, *Australian Interests in the Far East*; the sustained commentary favouring regionalism as an alternative to empire subservience from 1937 on in the *Austral–Asiatic Bulletin*; the symposia of the Australian Institute of International Affairs (AIIA) in the late 1930s on the challenges of modern nationalism in Asia[33]—all of these need to be recalled and, more pertinently, their similarities to the concerns of current governments must be acknowledged.

The Pacific War and habits of Cold War thinking accentuated negative images of Asia in Australian minds, from the 1940s to the 1960s. Forward defence and the engagement of Australian troops in Korea, Malaya and Vietnam further complicated our attitudes. Yet potential cooperative coexistence with governments of the region was not forgotten, as the then Minister for External Affairs, H V Evatt registered: '. . . the existence of stable, progressive, prosperous and democratically-inclined governments in the Pacific and Asia is fundamental to Australia's own security'.[34]

To recover this vein of sustained commentary on Asia is not to gainsay that in general the public ignorance concerning Asia was appalling. The issue, however, is not that the knowledge was not available, but why, for so long, it failed to become the concern of government, why it did not reach the policy agenda, why it did not become a theme in public education?

Asia, economics and imagination

To put it simply, Australia did not ignore Asia for so long because it was (in Evans' terms) 'Anglophonic and Anglophilic', but because there was no economic advantage for it to encourage a consciousness of its region. Far from standing outside the mainstream, it has for most of its history, 'occupied a side table in a revolving restaurant on top of the world'[35]—which is to say, the mainstream was entirely different. Recall its origins—Australia's real start came in the nineteenth century as a subsidiary part of the British economy, supplying staples to British industry. Most settler society economies remained specialist economies supplying larger markets elsewhere, and Australia was no exception.[36] It found difficulty in diversifying, and it has remained essentially a resource trading nation, looking towards world markets. It was a satellite of Britain until the Second World War, when Britain was still 'far and away Australia's largest trading partner and the largest overseas investor'.[37] Indeed, Carl Bridge shows that 'Australia had no real options outside the Empire'.[38]

Thereafter, despite Australia's 'salvation' by the USA in the Pacific War, it was nonetheless the case that 'in 1945, and for another quarter century, Britain came back into South East Asia and Australasia. It remained Australia's main trading and investment partner until the 1960s'.[39] If Britain was forced to retreat by economic circumstances in the 1960s, which dictated that it look to Europe, the ensuing American economic hegemony was short-lived. The United States dominance of investment in and trade with Australia lasted barely a decade. By the 1970s and 1980s the tide was already turning on American power: rival economies were growing and the US economy was faltering. Thus Japan replaced the US as Australia's major trading partner, and trade with other Asian nations rapidly grew.[40]

Is it any wonder that the British connection remained so prominent in the Australian national consciousness, that population links and cultural continuity were so taken-for-granted, and that geography was (relatively speaking) so ignored, so long as Australia remained tied to the imperial economy? And given that another 'great and powerful friend' in the US thereafter constituted the mainstream, is it any surprise that Asia should emerge so late as an object for Australian attention? Geography did not determine the mainstream, trade and investment did. In one sense, the 'crimson thread of kinship' might be taken as a metaphor for the trade and security interests of the past: is 'geography' any more than a metaphor for those interests in the present? The point is, as a settler economy, Australia has *never* stood aside from the mainstream: its policy makers have had to attempt to be alert to potential advantage in a larger market.

It must not be assumed (as some writers have) that Australia in these years had its head in the sand, was dependent on its allies' policy assessments and was not making decisions based on its own interests.[41]

Policy makers assessing Australia's economic interests could be forgiven for thinking (absolutely until the 1940s, in a more qualified sense until the 1960s) that they could turn their backs on the world outside Britain. Thereafter, there was advantage in pursuing the US connection. When these empires faltered and withdrew, then Australia had to diversify—and *Realpolitik* in the past twenty years has demanded an accommodation with Asia.

New enlightenment, or the same old strategy?

Changing circumstances demand new public education and attempts to transform the public culture. It's conventional to regard new policy approaches as evidence of increased enlightenment. Thus, policy makers of the present tend to berate us for having stood outside the mainstream (*pace* Evans), to talk of the new consensus as evincing maturity (*pace* Woolcott) and to pretend that no one before has taken a serious interest in Asia (despite one hundred years of contrary examples).

This is no more than rhetoric. It is as much a myth to say that Australians were preoccupied with Europe in the past *simply* because they were 'Anglophonic and Anglophilic' as it is to say geography is the only reality of the present. The enduring realities are economic advantage and security—which policy makers have always pursued.

Is it possible that the aggressively instrumental economic language of the present may actually work against cultural engagement? Of course we should engage with Asian countries, but our impulses should be curiosity, interest, openness to difference, a desire to learn. Public education in Australia should accentuate these, rather than hectoring us about economic survival. Equally the strong sense that every link is trade-driven does little justice to the growing networks of Asian scholars who have developed Australian studies purely out of interest and curiosity: what, they may well think, happens to them if the trade winds shift?

Even on the economic front, we are left with some questions. Is Australia's commitment to its region the spur to internationalising the economy? Or is the regional focus (for all that it encourages multilateralism rather than the bilateralism of former ties with Britain and the US) a blinker on a truly international perspective? In a world of instant financial transfers, efficient and swift long haul transportation and the information superhighway, might the 'neighbourhood' metaphor be a constraint on trade? Can we *both* foster Asian links, *and* remain alert to opportunities elsewhere? Or is this an instance of one big idea crowding out all other options? Are we aiming for the best of all worlds (where we'll have freedom of movement), or—just as in the past—tying our interests to the powerhouses of the moment?

What we have here is a case study of how closely the struggle over what is (or should be) central to national consciousness is tied to economic transitions.[42] Attitudes to the world outside Australia do not change because there has been a change in public opinion or self-regard. Rather, those whose concern is with government, seek to mould public opinion and national consciousness to serve what they see to be in the country's interests. The ideas that can be used to serve this purpose are always in play—Asia, as we saw, was never 'forgotten' by some among Australia's intelligentsia. But only in particular circumstances will a particular pattern of ideas come to the fore—thus, in our example, the importance of Asia and the demands of 'geography' serve the needs of the moment. An important role will be played by the intelligentsia—including government ministers and officials (such as Evans and Woolcott) and professional intellectuals (such as Garnaut). These people, while building on the scholarly work of the past, reinvent it as something new, attuned to unique problems which our forebears, we are encouraged to think, had been too limited to apprehend. Thus imperatives and prescriptions are generated, and the people are belaboured to take a fresh look at themselves and to wake up to present realities. So Australians are forever (and always for the first time) told we must fight our own battles, as we have always sought to do.[43]

CHAPTER 3

The message from 'the great elsewhere'—the end of history?

What exactly are the ideas that have become so dominant in Western polities as to blind us to the contradictions within our economies? Why are they so persuasive as to be taken up uncritically by 'reformers' in so-called 'developing' countries? What is the argument that makes them so attractive? And how have they become so taken-for-granted in general public understanding?

At the end of the 1980s, with communist states everywhere in retreat and Western consumer economies being promoted as models for the world, Francis Fukuyama published an article which expressed, better than anything else, the wisdom of the moment. It was called 'The End of History?'.[1] Fukuyama put into words what Western politicians and business leaders long felt they had 'known'. There was, on the one hand, excitement among those (and most politicians were among them) who 'recognised' Fukuyama's message. And there was, on the other hand, a body of agitated critics. The debate encouraged Fukuyama to extend his argument into a book, *The End of History and the Last Man*.[2] So quickly did the Fukuyama line become taken for granted, that one could find, for instance, then Australian foreign minister, Gareth Evans, repeating it both as an explanation for change in Asia, and as justification for Australia's strategy in Asian relations.[3] I take this as a manifestation of Fukuyama's brilliance in articulating the received wisdom. His is an argument, then, that tells us something essential about our times. But what did he say? History, according to Fukuyama, is the story of ideological evolution, and hence of ideological conflict. Each past society has claimed its ideal to be superior to another's, and this fuelled the narrative of conflict and development with which history was concerned. Now, however, we are seeing the 'unabashed victory of economic and political liberalism' and with it 'the total exhaustion of viable systematic alternatives to Western liberalism' and the 'ineluctable spread of consumerist Western culture'.[4]

What we are witnessing is in fact the end of history. There will be no change in the future because we have reached the end of ideological evolution and the universalisation of Western liberal democracy as the final form of human government. This realisation has been achieved because the only systematic alternatives to Western liberal forms have been fascism— which was defeated—and communism—which, we saw, failed comprehensively. Change comes with the victory of one idea over another, but now, in the absence of alternatives, there is only one idea, and one form of state:

> The state that emerges at the end of history is liberal insofar as it recognises and protects through a system of law man's universal right to freedom, and democratic insofar as it exists only with the consent of the governed . . . (H)uman history and the conflict that characterised it was based on the existence of 'contradictions' . . . But in the universal homogenous state, all prior contradictions are resolved and all human needs are satisfied . . . what remains is primarily economic activity.[5]

Are there no contradictions in Western liberal democracies that are unresolvable? Class, suggests Fukuyama, is a receding issue—the root causes of inequality are a legacy of pre-modern conditions, and there are no legal or structural features that sustain inequality in 'our society, which remains fundamentally egalitarian and moderately redistributionist'.[6] We may remain unhappy 'with the impersonality and spiritual vacuity of liberal consumerist societies . . . it is not at all clear that is remediable through politics'.[7]

Another contradiction not yet resolved by liberalism is that posed by nationalism—which has spawned the major cataclysms of the twentieth century, has threatened liberalism historically and remains a threat even in parts of 'post-historical' Europe. And yet we may hold out some hope because 'the vast majority of the world's nationalist movements . . . do not offer anything like a comprehensive agenda for socioeconomic organisation'.[8] This failure will allow the liberal idea to triumph.

It's important to stress that Fukuyama is arguing about the dominance of an idea, a particular form of consciousness. The ideal liberal society may not be achieved, and it is certain that not all societies will reach the same stage at the same time:

> But at the end of history it is not necessary that all societies become successful liberal societies, merely that they end their ideological pretensions of representing different and higher forms of human society.[9]

Economic advantage and progress in the liberal mode are explicitly linked by Fukuyama with the internationalisation of national markets. Control of the borders of the Eastern bloc made economic progress beyond a certain level impossible for the communist regimes, while intervention by elites in Latin America to maintain their privileged positions within national markets held those countries back. In contrast, the East Asian 'tiger' economies prospered because of their willingness to integrate with the world economy. For these countries, and for the West generally:

> the global division of labour . . . has become a reality . . .
> The continuing decrease in transportation and communication costs has resulted in the realization of economies of scale greater than were possible in even the largest national markets . . . The result has been . . . the unification of a very large part of mankind (outside the communist world) in a single market.[10]

In broad terms, the result is:

> . . . the creation of a universal consumer culture based on liberal economic principles . . . The enormously productive

and dynamic world created by advancing technology and the rational organization of labour has a tremendous homogenizing power. It is capable of linking different societies . . . physically through the creation of global markets, and of creating parallel economic aspirations and practices . . . The attractive power of this world creates a very strong *predisposition* for all human societies to participate.[11]

The dominance of the liberal idea will form universal modes of economic behaviour. The connection between liberal politics, and a liberal economy, has been flagged from the first (Fukuyama ties political practice to the spread of Western consumerism, as we see above). The universal modus operandi will be what he calls the 'Common Marketisation' of international relations (which he opposes to nineteenth century competitiveness).

In linking democratic politics and liberal economics Fukuyama is unpersuasive. At one point, ideas and consciousness are seen as more important than material considerations ('to understand the emergence of modern capitalism and the profit motive one had to study their antecedents in the realm of the spirit'[12]). Yet, at another point, the achievement of material benefits is said to be laying the ground for political democracy. ('The economic success of the . . . NICs in Asia . . . is . . . a familiar story . . . political liberalism has been following economic liberalism, more slowly than many had hoped but with seeming inevitability'.[13]) In the end, the interplay between 'free' politics and 'free and decentralized decision-making with respect to investment, labour and prices'[14] is simply assumed. What is made clear, however, is that 'the world that has reached the end of history is far more preoccupied with economics than with politics or strategy':

idealism will be replaced by economic calculation, the endless solving of technical problems, environmental concerns, and the satisfaction of sophisticated consumer demands
. . . [T]here will be neither art nor philosophy, just the perpetual caretaking of the museum of human history.[15]

I will return later to some perplexing issues in this argument—Can we so easily conflate politics and economics? Do there remain contradictions within liberalism that this argument simply can't resolve? Were fascism and communism the only challenges to liberal states? Has there been an unabashed victory of economic and political liberalism, or—in view of the problems reviewed in chapter 1—might we not equally talk of the exhaustion of liberal ideas?

First, however, I want to link Fukuyama's argument with one that has achieved wide circulation in Australia, and with similar effects, Paul Kelly's thesis in his book *The End of Certainty*.[16] Then I want to expand on why I take each of them to be expressive of their times, and why they achieved such credence.

Fukuyama offers an historical argument for the growing dominance of liberal economic ideas, increasing globalisation of markets and homogenisation of lifestyles and states (leading to diminishing differences in politics, and so in polities—hence the end of history). In comparison, Kelly provides a case study of the process in action. Kelly's book was written at the same time as, rather than as a response to, Fukuyama's: evidence that each speaks for the historical moment.

Kelly argues that Australia built an industrial economy not on free market principles but in terms of a bipartisan consensus that relied on a favoured trading position in a larger empire ('imperial benevolence'), and involved strategies— immigration restriction, industry protection, wage arbitration and state paternalism—which depended on an interventionist state.[17] None of this is new: Hancock and Eggleston advanced similar arguments in the 1930s, before the (protected) industrial boom of the 1950s and 1960s.[18] But Kelly provides a skilful historical synthesis of what he evocatively calls 'the Australian settlement'. The burden of his argument, however, is to describe where and why the 'settlement' went wrong in the 1980s, and then to suggest that it was always misconceived (and that it had been seen to be so by enlightened 'free-traders', like George Reid, eighty years ago).

What caused the collapse of the ideas which Australia had embraced at Federation was economic crisis. A deep malaise in the 1980s forced us to recognise that the state's role (through protection, wage regulation, paternalistic welfare)

had stifled market potential. Australia, a leader in most mea-
/sures of economic wellbeing at the turn of the century, had
steadily slid down the league table ever since. Finally, the
strategies that had constituted the Australian settlement could
not survive the weakening of Australia's 'imperial' links with
its two patrons, Britain and the USA. And the 'recognition that
commodity prices were deteriorating relative to other prices;
that Australia had to diversify its export base while exploiting
natural comparative advantage; and that low protection was
the route to integration with the high-growth economies of
the Asia–Pacific'.[19] Just as both sides of politics had worked
within the parameters of the Australian settlement, groups on
both sides now accept the need to diversify, internationalise
and deregulate.

The major difference is between such free market purists
as John Hewson and the more pragmatic approach of Bob
Hawke and Paul Keating. In the early 1990s 'the real division
in Australian politics was horizontal, a split running through
all parties that separated market-orientated reformers from
state power traditionalists'.[20] Free-market reform, however,
will be irresistible: it is driven by politics, technology and
intellectual force and it is a global phenomenon not unique to
Australia[21] (a point that Fukuyama's pronouncements from the
great Elsewhere reinforce). In sum:

> The decade of the 1980s saw the advance towards a
> multicultural Australia, the demise of Protection, the start of
> the long-waited assault on Arbitration, a loss of confidence in
> state power and a turning away from government
> paternalism, a shift towards market power and deregulation
> . . . efforts to secure better enterprise productivity and
> workplace reform, a deeper sense of national self-reliance, a
> reappraisal of welfare as a need not a right, and an emphasis
> on individual responsibility as well as individual entitlement.
> Australia's economic orientation was more outward-looking
> and its aspiration was to become an efficient and confident
> nation in the Asia/Pacific.[22]

The transition to 'an economy geared to a new test of
international competition, a greater reliance upon markets to
set prices . . . a growing emphasis on individual skills and

enterprise productivity . . .'[23] has not yet been fully achieved, but, warns Kelly, the lesson is to perfect the transition from a closed to an open economy. The mistake would be to retreat. And once the transition is achieved?

> Post-protectionist Australia will be subject to powerful international forces—the world economy is becoming more global; financial markets are global; product markets are relatively open despite the influence of protection; huge deregulated labour markets operate in America and the Asia/Pacific; the European community will become one vast labour market; the 'trade-in-services' provisions of the GATT round recognize the greater freedom of international movement; technology and communications are destroying national borders. In this climate the task of national economic policy will be to create a setting for efficiency and productivity; to make Australia a proposition for overseas investment for competitive industry. This means that workforces which are overpaid by world standards will not maintain their jobs.[24]

The last two sentences of this passage make clear that in this brave new world, where all our old certainties have been swept away, Australia's strategy must be exactly that recommended by Sir Otto Niemeyer in 1930 (see chapter 1). Some certainties, then, don't change.

Fukuyama and Kelly express the wisdom of the moment with a comprehensiveness and historical sweep that gives it real force. They address real problems—Kelly, for instance, is surely right in arguing that Australia's economic crisis ends the old certainties. And, in offering firm answers in a time of flux and doubt, they cater to the needs of a wide audience. That may be why they seem to have achieved the last word on their topics.

Or is it that they have given a rationale, dignity (and hard covers) to those arguments that are the stuff of daily media recapitulation? For instance, a series of articles by the economics editor of *The Australian*, Alan Wood, in 1994, made these propositions: that Australia's future hinges on a renewed commitment to lifting our competitiveness; that globalisation of the economy alone offers the potential for higher standards of living; that we must be careful not to blame globalisation for current economic ills since these are caused by declines in productivity and competitiveness; and that if Western nations can sustain the confidence to continue liberalising trade, Asia and Eastern Europe can be peacefully integrated into the world economy and we can look forward to the achievement of global prosperity in the next century.[25] Similar points were made by economic commentators in all mainstream media in late 1993 to support the North American Free Trade Agreement (NAFTA), APEC and the General Agreement on Tariffs and Trade (GATT) round. Indeed, there was no dissenting voice in the mass media, with the exception of Ken Davidson of the *Age*.

The consensus among economic commentators might suggest (if we assume Davidson is simply idiosyncratic) that the logic of these arguments is inescapable. This might seem clear evidence for Fukuyama's central proposition: that there is no other tenable idea left in the field of debate—we must address problems as problems of management within liberal free market economies because this is all that is left. This mindset dominates because it assumes the logic of inevitability. It finds an audience because, at a time of turmoil, it answers our need for clear directions. It attracts because we are all assumed to benefit with global prosperity (as one headline had it, 'Capitalism to the rescue and no losers'[26]). The obverse, though, is a message that plays on our anxieties: we may be 'stifled' by the past, or left behind as the 'poor white trash' of Asia, or fail to maintain our jobs, if we can't compete. In time the mindset becomes virtually the sole message broadcast in public discussion. Is the relentlessness and ubiquity of the argument, however, enough to completely allay the concerns raised in chapter 1? Can those cases be explained entirely as problems of transition, or even (in isolated cases) of market failure? Markets do fail, Kelly disarmingly concedes:

> . . . markets are not perfect and do not necessarily advance the national interest. The realistic free market reformers never pretended that markets were perfect; they just said that markets, on balance, would deliver a better result than governments.[27]

But what about those who are landed with paying for Canary Wharf, or travelling on London Transport, or trying to maintain order in Hungary, or developing democracy in Russia, or living in Bridgeport? Doesn't the range of their problems suggest more systematic blindspots in these theories?

CHAPTER 4

Problems with the message

Where do Fukuyama and Kelly go wrong? In my view, both of them re-read the past in anachronistic ways. Consider Fukuyama's motive: he is arguing for a universal, directional history, and must present a story that accounts for the triumph of 'the liberal idea', and of the system that is said to flow from that idea—the free market. Undoubtedly, he reflects the form of liberalism that dominates contemporary public debate. It is another matter whether the present 'moment' can be so confidently read back into the past: to do so is to ignore the complexity of the liberal tradition in which 'ameliorative' or social liberalism has played a powerful role.

Individualist liberals—of whom Fukuyama is a contemporary example—argue that freedom means the liberty to exercise choice without hindrance by the state. Social liberals argue that the state must ensure that minimal conditions are satisfied to make free choice meaningful: you aren't free to choose if you're constrained by poverty, for instance.

Individualists regard the state as an unfortunate necessity—necessary to maintain order, but to be kept as small as possible, with limited functions, and always open to challenge. They assume that if state power is not constantly challenged, it will draw more and more to itself and impinge on the rights of individuals freely to choose.

Social liberals argue that the community owes a duty of care towards each of its members, so that if unregulated free markets produce unemployment, for instance, the state should provide a safety net to 'ameliorate' the worst effects of this outcome, to raise the disadvantaged to the position where they can still make meaningful choices. This is the rationale that led to the modern welfare state—the institutions of which are under siege today.

Fukuyama's insistence that politics can be reduced to the ideological divisions between 'world systems'—communism, fascism and liberal democracy—obscures the fact that in most Western polities the political battles have been bound up with these differences in liberalism. Indeed, he would deprive us of a meaningful political history *within* the varieties of liberal polity (such as Australia, or the US). This is because we often understand the characteristics of a specific society to depend upon its balance between the opposed tendencies of liberalism (Australia's supposed 'bush legend', for instance, is an argument about a collectivist rather than an individualist ethos). Fukuyama flattens out all differences—he sees only one form of liberalism—and so could destroy our sense of historical community. Fukuyama is, after all, intent on describing the homogenisation of the liberal world.[1]

Kelly's anachronism—and emptying of political history—is even clearer. His astute description of 'the Australian settlement' shows the ameliorative tendency,[2] and the expectation of a significant role by the state,[3] to be leading characteristics in Australian politics. The difficulty emerges when he implies that, because such assumptions no longer seem appropriate, they were always mistaken. Thus, the tactics which generated a local politics and sustained an economy increasingly oriented to Australian interests can be shrugged off as simply 'the protectionist shackles which stifled its (Australia's) first century'.[4] How such delusions could have survived, with (to some extent) bipartisan support and popular acceptance, is a mystery. That there might be some cause for pride in Australia's political achievement is inconceivable.

Australia's history in the world economy

Kelly is wrong on the very ground on which he stakes his claim—an understanding of world capitalism. None of the industrialising economies of the nineteenth and twentieth centuries ever relied on the free market alone. In this context, Australia's protectionism was neither isolated nor eccentric. More importantly, Australia has always been integrated into a world market as I suggest in chapter 2, but that market was differently organised in the past. The history of free settlement and of investment in Australia between 1815 and 1945 must be understood in terms of Australia's role in the British sphere of the world economy. That has certainly changed since the 1940s, with America, then Japan, and more lately Asia, becoming the foci of Australian trade and investment. But the key point is that, until the 1970s, though capitalist interests have long been transnational, the principal sites of capital formation were within nation states.

While Australia's modern economy was developing, there was intense rivalry between the major industrial powers (Britain, Germany and the USA). There were sustained attempts to coordinate world markets by these powers, but through consolidated industrialisation within nation states, characterised by high levels of protection. These elements were not necessarily in contradiction. In the Australian case, for instance, as Peter Cochrane has shown,[5] the economy was first organised around production of staples for export, geared to the demands of the British market. Later—from the late nineteenth century—urbanisation and industrialisation were stimulated by redistribution within the British empire in response to declining British fortunes in other parts of the world. Australian industrial growth was to be integrated with and dependent upon British technology, while still dependent on British investment and an expanding export surplus to pay off interest charges. Britain's loss of export markets gave rise to an imperial policy aimed at the efficient reallocation of capital and labour within the empire.[6] Import replacement was part of the strategy of coordinated industrial development, with, after 1930, a shift of British investment from securities to manufacturing.[7]

Britain's maintenance of an empire was much weakened by the Second World War, but it remained Australia's main trading and investment partner until the 1960s. Thereafter, the USA dominated—pouring in capital and new technology, but on condition that US companies could establish subsidiaries behind the import controls and tariff barriers intended to generate a diversified ecohomy within Australia.

A striking instance of the pattern was the rapid growth of an Australian car manufacturing industry, dominated by US giants, General Motors and Ford. American dominance lasted little more than a decade. Japanese investment followed American. 'From being an appendage of one, Australia had graduated economically to a field for the play of forces from several of the international centres of capitalism.'[8] This of course was part of a bigger picture, the reconstruction of capitalist economies after the war, which continued to involve major metropolitan players and new institutions for international regulation such as the International Monetary Fund, alongside the reinforcement of national economies through protectionist measures.

Little wonder, then, that Australia's integration into the world economy took the form it did until the 1970s. Far from being introverted and 'stifled' as Kelly would have us believe, Australian policy makers might well have turned the pattern of what looked like dependency to national advantage. Kosmas Tsokhas, for instance, analysing the wool industry between the wars, argues that economic nationalism, rather than empire loyalty, drove Australian politicians and trade negotiators, and that they achieved power and autonomy in the relationship with the imperial centre.[9] Carl Bridge insists that Australia did not simply follow its allies in post-war years, but made realistic assessments of its own interests.[10] And a range of commentators, to whom I return in chapter 6, have argued that the economic policies Kelly derides were a sensible path to nation-building in the context of the world economy of the time.[11]

Indeed, surely it is only the fact that they were relatively productive in their own terms that can explain the sustenance of such approaches over seventy years? If these conditions did not endure, it was *not* because Australia, uniquely, had lost the plot, but because the circumstances of world capitalism changed, and changed radically.

Liberal internationalism and the present

Consider the premise—explicit in Fukuyama, implicit in Kelly—that the present is shaped by the triumph of an idea, and that idea triumphs because it works. What if, instead, our present is shaped by structural changes in world capitalism since the 1970s—changes flowing from a reconfiguration in the world market (in which ideas were largely irrelevant)? Would this suggest a different logic? Does a structural explanation provide a better account of the gaps between promise and outcome introduced in chapter 1?

The early 1970s saw an end to what had been, since the mid–1940s, one of the most stable expansions ever experienced in the world economy. There were specific shocks. The OPEC oil crisis, for instance, dramatically skewed the cost of energy inputs in most economies and politicised commodity trading. As those countries least able to manage their balance of payments (because of the hike in oil prices) turned to the IMF and other international agencies, these agencies could impose their free market ideology (help was conditional on accepting the deregulatory prescription). The geopolitical balance which underlay economic growth was disturbed. US power, once essential in the post-war reorganisation of the capitalist economies, was significantly diminished. The US was forced to withdraw from Vietnam, it confronted industries in Western Europe and Japan that were by then fully competitive with and sometimes more 'efficient' than US industries. The Cold War 'balance' that had underwritten US dominance was already starting to unravel, not only because of Vietnam but also because the so-called socialist bloc was in disarray— Chinese and Soviet policy was at odds, and the USSR's relations with its Eastern European allies were becoming difficult.

All this was linked with a serious economic downturn. Many competitors emerged to challenge the relative monopolies of affluent producer nations. Profit rates declined. High rates of unemployment (and hence reduced demand) resulted. Politicised competition in a tighter world market drove increased concentration of capital, geographical relocation of production, and a search for constant innovation.[12]

The period when a few major metropolitan players could manage capital formation within nation states in a climate of stability guaranteed by US dominance was ending. What followed was that the agents of capital accumulation (e.g. transnational companies) and the mechanisms that made it possible (e.g. financial markets) were divorced from the 'politicising' distortions of the nation state.

Theories of liberal internationalism argue that the 1970s forced us to recognise the limits of regulation within nations: we all had to 'free-up', and those nations which most rapidly deregulated and integrated into an international free market would most rapidly recover. The pressure behind structural change, however, was not the liberal ideal, but new strategies for corporate survival: 'Technological change, automation, the search for new product lines and market niches, geographical dispersal to zones of easier labour control, mergers and steps to accelerate the turnover time of . . . capital surged to the fore . . . '[13] Remarkable advances in technology added momentum: transport became faster, cheaper and more efficient; satellites allowed instant worldwide electronic communication; computers facilitated rapid analysis; technical design and scientific knowledge could be speedily assessed and disseminated.

If smart entrepreneurialism drew on all of these developments, the most fundamental change issuing from new technologies was 'the complete reorganization of the global financial system and the emergence of greatly enhanced powers of financial coordination'[14]—but powers that rested with financial markets rather than nation states. This system is enormously complicated, and has 'eluded any collective control on the part of even the most powerful capitalist states'.[15] Indeed:

> . . . the new financial systems put into place since 1972 have changed the balance of forces at work in the global capitalist system, giving much more autonomy to the banking and financial system relative to corporate, state and personal financing . . . The increasing powers of co-ordination lodged within the world's financial system have emerged . . . at the expense of the nation state to control capital flow and, hence, its own fiscal and monetary policy . . . Since that time all nation states have been at the mercy of financial disciplining either through the effects of capital flow . . . or by direct institutional disciplining.[16]

Are the 'parallel practices' Fukuyama discerns in the 'common marketization' of international life, then, really the manifestation of a shared idea? Or are they a result of market disciplines that maintain 'a single "world" where none previously existed'?[17] And do they produce a world with richer possibilities for autonomous choice?

Free markets, employment and choice

Meaningful choices only exist in an environment that offers options. There must be alternative options relating to employment, to cultural goods, and to discretionary use of income. These must be supported by relative stability (economic and social), and protection against extremes of inequity or privation that would hamper any choices at all.

On each of these matters, the potential outcome of liberal internationalism is problematic. Competition, efficiency, flexibility in an international context do not necessarily translate into more jobs in a particular community. The de-industrialisation of economies like Australia or Britain or the US is a consequence of the ability of international firms to maintain headquarters, management, decision-making (and profits) in their 'home' countries, but to reduce labour costs by shifting production to low wage-rate peripheral countries. Hence the death of cities like Bridgeport, and the turmoil in the Australian labour market—which has been the subject of extensive commentary here by left and right.[18]

Even more significant may be economic strategies within advanced economies. The corporate 'downsizing', for instance, that is equated with 'efficiency' may undermine the economy: when one company gains a competitive edge by doing more with less, it achieves greater productivity. But when an entire economy works that way, the income lost to displaced workers may outweigh the gains to productivity. Indeed, the job losses and wage cuts that flow from technological improvements and a change in organisational ethos may be more to do with competition within and between rich countries than with labour redistribution from rich to poor countries.[19] Yet most people within Western societies are dependent on wage labour. In the current circumstances, they see their options reduced (or disappearing); the stability conducive to the diligence and self-improvement said to be part of the capitalist ethos diminishing; and the thing that provides life satisfaction and a self-identity—steady work—an uncertain prospect.

Disruption to labour markets has direct effects on income inequality, with disastrous social effects. In Britain, during the 1980s, there was the greatest increase in the inequality of income distribution in Europe. During the same period, Britain suffered the most rapid increase in the incidence of crime in Europe. The growth in the inequality of disposable incomes strongly correlated with the increase in crime. Clearly criminals feel no stake in the society in which they find themselves; no responsibility, that is, to the collective.

Is it too much to suggest that the increase in criminality is linked with the transition to a market society, with a consequent decline in the sense of community and a rise in anonymity? And in the areas where the disadvantaged have most direct contact with the state, the privatisation of public infrastructure has signalled a retreat from universal standards—still further fragmentation to reinforce alienation. Far from seeing the need to recover social cohesion, and to explore the links between social conditions and civil disorder, the response of the British government has been to attempt tougher policing, with the paradoxical outcome that alongside the 'free market' the state has poured more and more funding into a futile attempt to regulate 'individual' morality.[20]

For those lucky enough to remain in work, has the 'freeing-up' of the financial sector offered appreciable advantages? Well, the deregulation of Australian banking has been a mixed blessing.[21] Deregulation was to encourage new players, to make existing banks lift their games in response to competition, to impel better investment decisions as a means of keeping an edge, to drive down interest rates—to provide a better service to the Australian customer. Instead, there was little change in who were the big players: the old oligopoly went on as before. Far from promoting wise investment, there were splurges of ill-judged credit, with no productive outcomes. The banks were central in the ruinous careers of the corporate buccaneers of the 1980s, with devastating effects on the national debt. Interest rates went up. The supposed effects of a competitive banking regime have not been achieved. Indeed, some argue that deregulation-induced movements in capital and credit placed such pressures on interest rates and foreign debt as to exacerbate the recession in Australia.[22]

In chapter 1, I noted that when deregulated banks made mistakes (as with London's Docklands), the community bore the cost (through higher interest rates, and restrictions on loans). Turning things over to markets does not move the risks from the community at large to entrepreneurs prepared to gamble on such risks, as some of the British attempts to privatise public utilities make clear. The fate of the British coal industry and the strategy for privatising electricity production provide one example.

Competition in electricity was to be achieved by splitting up the nationally integrated electricity generating system, and selling off the regions to competing producers. No entrepreneurs could be found prepared to buy into the nuclear power industry because of the enormous long-term costs of decommissioning plant. While attempts continued to privatise coal mining (coal powered generators were, with nuclear plants, the major components of national base-load production), it was decided that the new regional producers would be required to take base-load from the national nuclear- and coal-powered electricity grid, but could achieve their 'competitive edge' by making their own decisions concerning variable peak loads. Gas turbine electricity generation provided an efficient means of generating such loads for small regional producers, and gas was cheaper than coal. But most producers calculated that they could reduce costs by minimising reliance on the national grid and building up capacity, through their own generators. The demand for coal fell. Coal stockpiles built up: an industry geared to national electricity generation was suddenly massively 'over-producing'. There was no European market for the British surplus.

The government decided to close pits, sacrificing scores of thousands of jobs, and decimating mining communities. The more pits closed, the less attractive the British coal industry became to corporate buyers. Meanwhile, gas production—faced with higher levels of demand than predicted—had to be cranked up, and the reaction was typical of 'the market' facing high demand: prices were increased. Regional gas turbine electricity generation—once the cheap option—became more expensive than the coal and nuclear-powered national grid had been. But regional producers had made their investments, and in the end the consumers simply had to pay. The 'experts' behind the privatisation of British electricity production resurfaced in late 1994 as the chief advisers to the Victorian premier, Jeff Kennett, in the planned privatisation of electricity generation there.

A similarly dysfunctional prospect loomed with the continuing attempts to privatise British Rail (a process not finalised at the time of writing). A unified national system was to be broken up into twenty-five 'shadow' franchises and more than eighty new companies. There were five problems. First, private companies appeared less likely to engage with each other in open competition than to attempt to achieve monopolies on the profitable inter-city routes, leaving the 'unprofitable' lines to close down. Second, under the new system, there was no guarantee that travellers could 'book through' on a single ticket through the jungle of routes that would emerge. Third, preparation for privatisation was to draw, it was said, £200 million from a system in which there had been serious underinvestment for a decade. Fares would have to rise to meet these costs (the burden of the expense would be borne by taxpayers and commuters, not by the potential buyers). Fourth, shareholders of private corporations would likely demand higher dividends than governments do, leading to yet higher fares just to create profits before companies could consider fresh investment. The problems of underinvestment would therefore continue. Fifth, unlike electricity, however, which few can do without, rail travel can be avoided as commuters turn instead to cheaper car and coach travel (travel choice, you will note, is becoming more rather than less limited)—exacerbating road congestion, city pollution, and travel delays. The expectation—that privatisation generates competition, lower prices and increased efficiency— is likely to be confounded, producing a rail service that is disaggregated, less comprehensive, less efficient in transporting people and goods, and vastly more expensive than what preceded it.[23]

What about the choice of cultural goods in an international market? In the concluding negotiations of the 1993 GATT round, the French television and film industries argued strongly against deregulation in the cultural area since US dominance of audio-visual media would constrain choice—in particular, the choice of product from the local culture. The free market response (and virtually the sole response in the Australian press) was that this was nonsense: a free market in cultural goods gave people potentially infinite choice, and if they chose to consume the American product, then so be it. But how accurate is this?

In relation to Australian television, John Docker has defended the free market in cultural production.[24] He attacks the elitist position that an enlightened minority could know (and should dictate, through state instrumentalities) what people should see But that was not the *only* element in the initial argument for regulation: people were also intent on preserving a corner for the community *against* the market. They were not so much dictating the content of what was produced in that corner, but allowing that there might be a space for production not constrained by market imperatives:[25]

> The intention of the Australian content regulations has been to encourage diverse Australian production rather than to impose 'higher' forms of culture . . . It does not seem unreasonable that an independent agency should establish minimum guidelines to encourage local cultural production in order to ensure that national culture remains vibrant and relevant.[26]

Docker would respond that the most popular shows inevitably reflect the tastes and values of ordinary people:

> [T]o be popular in a majority sense, programs and the overall 'collective drama', the overall tone and feel of commercial stations have to appeal to popular traditions . . . If stations didn't put on programs that were popular they would financially fail—what could be more obvious?[27]

What does this reveal about markets? Docker's argument would apply if there was an infinite choice in the market, if it did offer everything. But is any market like this, and what does popularity mean when the choice is limited, when—as happened in the early years of Australian television—there is nothing relating to the vernacular culture on offer?

Would we accept Docker's argument if, say, it applied to the purchase of domestic chairs? Imagine, if you will, that you live in a small town. You decide one day that you need to buy a lounge chair. There are only two furniture stores. You visit both. One carries a line of plain wooden kitchen chairs. The other stocks an upright padded chair. Neither carries any sort of lounge chair because, you are told, 'there is no demand'. You opt for the padded chair as being closest to what you want, buy it, and go home feeling frustrated. Unknown to you, there is a small factory on the outskirts of town specialising in lounge furniture, which once supplied both shops. But the local shopkeepers found that they could import upright chairs at substantially lower unit costs from Taiwan, where labour costs are cheaper. The local manufacturer, unable to match these prices, could no longer place his product with the local shops. There is, the shopkeepers 'know', no upmarket client base in town. But they are happy—everybody is buying the chairs. So the market works. Is it lampooning Docker to say that this is exactly how his argument functions?

Such an argument depends on an unsophisticated view of the modern transnational market place—indeed, of the commercial nature of high modernity. For Docker, markets are the best means to serve libertarian ends, since they are most directly responsive to choice. But to believe that choice is 'open' is to ignore the fact that control of the technologies and marketing of product for the new popular media did not and could not remain within national boundaries. The process inevitably was part of transnational capitalism. As Raymond Williams said of the new visual media, 'many attempts were made to preserve at least domestic corporations, but the paranational scale significantly overbore them. The road to Hollywood was then . . . inscribed'.[28]

The practical point is that the political and commercial choices surrounding the introduction of television in Australia led to a very limited set of program options, dictated by the financial considerations of commercial telecasters (rather than by responses to public choice), and that in consequence audiences were formed within the bounds of those options. In that context, questions remain about whether public preferences could ever be fully expressed. Did what was produced have any but the most tenuous links with 'the people'? And might we not say that the attraction of audiences to Australian film and television now has been achieved only because regulation of the market allowed the space for Australian forms to flourish?

Liberal internationalism and newly industrialising countries

Instead of looking only at the impact of internalisation within countries like Australia, shouldn't we look at the opening up of choice across the world—especially as a result of development in the newly industrialising countries? Look, for instance, at the General Agreement on Tariffs and Trade (GATT), sponsored by the US in 1947 to encourage international free trade, and one of the key mechanisms in organising the post-war world market. Its aim has always been to remove tariff barriers, to reduce protection. The Uruguay round of the GATT negotiations, which began in Uruguay in 1986 and concluded in Geneva in December 1993, it was said, could not be allowed to fail lest the world sink into a welter of bilateral protectionism and trade wars. The director-general of GATT insisted that movement to a liberal trading order paralleled the world movement to democracy, even though conceding that it was 'undeniable that competition has adverse effects for the inefficient' and that there would have to be 'clear policies that stimulate employment' to soak up the job losses competition might induce.[29] (So purposeful state initiatives would have to underwrite world free trade?)

In the event, the conclusion of the GATT round was generally deemed a 'success'. Within months, however, bilateral trade conflict had broken out between the US and Japan and within a year significant reservations were expressed by the new Republican dominated US congress, undercutting the supposed commitment to free trade and suggesting that the biggest players will abide by such accords only to the extent that they suit their purposes. Australia will benefit in the medium term if the GATT agreement holds.[30]

The consequences, for the least advantaged parts of the world, are more ambiguous. One of the requirements of the latest accord is that developing countries deregulate their markets and remove controls on foreign investment—including controls on profit repatriation—thus eroding their ability to regulate foreign investment in a manner consistent with their development priorities.[31] So the power of international finance will be further advanced, and the autonomy of local and regional ways of life will be further undermined.

While a World Trade Organization has been established to police the accord (with anti-dumping regulations, for example) the absence of minimum social, environmental and economic standards will shift investment and jobs to those places with the lowest production costs, exercising a downward pressure on standards and the quality of life everywhere.[32] And, when it comes to the nitty gritty, two-thirds of the benefits will accrue to the developed countries of the West and the objects of their special attention (China in particular, and the 'tiger' economies of Asia in general) while the desperately disadvantaged countries of Africa will be net losers.[33]

The GATT process aside, is the transfer of prosperity from the developed to the developing world a 'win-win' situation, as our press frequently reports? The fact that the most successful Asian economies look set to achieve a distribution of income approximately that achieved in countries like Britain and Australia is deemed evidence that increasing prosperity has not been captured by elites.[34]

But the model is dubious: we saw that the maldistribution of income in Britain has had disastrously adverse effects on that country's social fabric. In addition, in the 'developing' world, traditional communities are displaced as traditional agriculture is scrapped to make way for cash crops to pay for development. The displaced flock to the cities, where there is insufficient urban infrastructure, and so a demand for new capital expenditure is generated—which these countries cannot afford. So emerge the shanty-towns, and a substantial, poorly-resourced underclass. Traditional values are swept away:

> economic value requires disvaluing all other forms of social existence, changing skills into lacks, commons into resources, men and women into commodified labour, tradition into burden, wisdom into ignorance, autonomy into dependency.[35]

In time, the monoculture of the West makes alternatives to the industrial growth orientated society unthinkable. The cultural dominance of the West makes people feel diminished: ' . . . in the villages . . . the excitement of life was here and now . . . people did not feel that they were on the periphery; the centre was where they were . . . The idealized stars of TV made people feel they were on the periphery, inferior and passive'.[36]

When such people gravitate to the cities in hope of the benefits of progress—decent jobs and high wages—they find low wages, no housing, no medical benefits and no job security.[37] The cost reductions afforded by low wage, labour-intensive, export oriented industries after all are precisely what has attracted foreign investment to those countries. Meanwhile, as capital is 'exported' from the developed economies (seeking minimal labour costs elsewhere), these economies are 'importing' unemployment, with large social costs. The 'new' service industries, it's argued, will take up the slack, but even these are showing substantial transfers of employment to low-cost areas.[38] (I am struck by this example: the British *Dictionary of National Biography*—a national institution—is being converted to electronic form, on CD-ROM, by keyboard operators in India.) And so the single world of liberal internationalism turns.

The need for new solutions

It is possible to conceive of a retort to each of the cases discussed: that nation states suffer because they do not try hard enough to achieve competitiveness (that is the constant lament in Australia); that international inequities are a transitional phase on the way to a more perfectly functioning world economy; that distortions arise because states persist with the delusion that they can intervene in their own interests; that the questions that concern me result from a failure of interpretation or inadequate economic knowledge. It is also possible that the freeing up of markets nationally and internationally will generate more wealth creation. I am not persuaded that this will generate more choices, or that it will solve the problems of distribution and relative wellbeing for all within nations, or even that it will achieve genuine global prosperity—though some people and some countries will do very well indeed.

Most of the benefits understood to be characteristic of the West—relative abundance, choice with security, maintenance of a meaningful identity within an autonomous community— seem now to be characteristics of the era of ameliorative liberalism when economic development depended upon a partnership between the state (acting for the community at large) and business enterprise (creating wealth). That era had its origins in the nineteenth century recognition that free trade led to social misery (witness the factory acts, and all that followed), but it also coincided with the era when capital formation took place within the nation state, and hence was more directly susceptible to political control. That era has passed: we cannot go back.

Yet the problems discussed here suggest that we must find newly relevant means of defining and asserting the interests of particular geo-political communities. It will not be enough to address the economic difficulties that we have seen to plague the new 'single World', nor to lament the cultural impact of the new monoculture—though each of these is essential. We must recognise that the process of pursuing our interests is, above all, a political process.

A real commitment to politics, as the ground for mediating between the social and the economic spheres, is now more important than ever. Yet such politics requires ideas, imagination and genuine competition between coherent alternatives, and this is what the triumph of the liberal ideal (in its current incarnation) denies us. Where there is only one idea, as Fukuyama rightly points out, 'idealism will be replaced by economic calculation, the endless solving of technical problems . . . and the satisfaction of sophisticated consumer demands . . . there will be neither art nor philosophy . . .'[39] The greatest problem with accepting the message of liberal internationalism is not that it fails to deliver the material advances that are promised in ways that satisfy the needs of the community. Rather, the greatest problem is that once we abandon politics for economics, we abandon the capacity to imagine new solutions.

CHAPTER 5

The failure of
political imagination

> . . . even when they became discontented, as they sometimes
> did, their discontent led nowhere, because, being without
> general ideas, they could only focus on specific grievances.

George Orwell, 1984

What have been the effects on practical politics of the mindset I describe in earlier chapters? What has been its impact, not on economic change and the politicking about it (which Kelly describes), but on the ways in which we think about ourselves and our options? What latitude has it allowed for recognition of difference and negotiation of diverse ends? How fruitful has it been in stimulating ideas which point to new futures? If you review the political history of the past twenty years in terms of such questions, you confront a 'shutdown'.[1] What is the malaise behind this?

Living in Britain at the time of the 1992 national elections, and back in Australia shortly before the 1993 federal elections, I had a good opportunity for comparison. What struck me were certain similarities. In both countries, there were tired governments, albeit of different complexions. Each had been in power too long, and many of their accomplishments were discredited. Yet there was anxiety about change, allowing for fears to be mobilised and encouraging populism. In each case there was the return of a government which few felt deserved to win (and most had predicted would not win). People felt that there were simply no options.[2] In 1996, Australia's conservative Coalition wrested power from Labor without an integrated platform, but with a promise to do nothing radical.

What has led to such dispiriting outcomes, to the sense that we are in a blind alley in which the only choice is that of the least unpalatable alternative? Policy particularities aside, what has led to the emptying of substance from political debate—the substance of policy agendas driven by ideas of a better future (let alone a 'vision' incorporating a moral order)?

Our popular understanding of politics often depends on leaders, what they represent and what they speak for. So let us approach this problem through the question: are there particular elements in the nature of political leadership over the past decade that illuminate the underlying malaise?

Great men in history? Hawke, Keating and destiny

The ALP government (1983–1996), has been popularly described in terms of the Hawke–Keating ascendancy—until their celebrated split in June 1991—and as in thrall to Keating after his assumption of the prime ministership in December 1991. The dynamics of their domination are well explained elsewhere,[3] but what do they actually represent?

Since the 1940s most political leaders have spoken for what Kelly has called 'the Australian settlement'. That is, they saw a role for the state in economic development and believed in politics as the ground for mediating between the social and the economic spheres. Robert Menzies' imaginative appeal to 'the forgotten people' in 1942 cast his audience as poised between 'the Socialist State, with its subordination of the individual to the universal officialdom of government', and 'the rich and powerful . . . who control great funds and enterprises, and are . . . able to protect themselves—though . . . in a political sense they have . . . shown neither comprehension nor competence'.[4]

The moral ground—the ground for politics—therefore lay between the state, and economic elites. Gough Whitlam believed the best ends could be achieved only by governments, and (echoing Hancock's observation forty years earlier) argued that a 'permanent aspect of our Australian society . . . is that . . . our demands for action always turn into demands for Government action, for Government assistance'.[5] Malcolm Fraser made much of the rhetoric of small government, but what emerged from a study of his prime ministership[6] and was clear in his later newspaper columns, was his belief in the politics of balancing markets and social needs:

> Deregulators . . . say that all government regulations are bad. A balanced approach, however, will recognize where regulation is necessary . . . it will also recognize when a regulation is damaging to economic activity. There is no universal rule . . . A deregulated system that leads to the highest international debt and unemployment we have had in 60 years . . . must surely cause policy-makers to ask questions . . . How long will it be before they understand that Australian Government must be more nationalistic in its policies?[7]

These leaders believed in the legitimacy of politics as inherently tied to its mediating role between what was essential to create economic growth and what was needed to protect the broader interests of the community. Every leader, up to and including Fraser, worried about and traded in ideas. Menzies spent the early 1940s reformulating his philosophy, through writing scripts for weekly radio broadcasts, and came up with his brilliant 'forgotten people' speech; Chifley condensed the constituents of Labor belief in his elaboration of the 'light on the hill'; Whitlam explored the foundation of the Australian settlement in a book on Labor and the constitution; and Fraser's ideas were collected in a book on Australia.[8] In each case, these leaders worked with ideas about the people, the sort of society they believed in, and the political means of achieving such a society. Theirs were essays in persuasion. With Hawke and Keating we enter a world where such possibilities can no longer be imagined.

We can plot the transition through the changes in Bob Hawke's own rhetoric. He starts, at least, with ideas. His attempt at a social and political vision, *The Resolution of Conflict*,[9] was written before he entered parliament. Thereafter, it was largely left behind (except for his subsequent stress on reconciliation and consensus), and it is nowhere mentioned in *The Hawke Memoirs*. Stan Anson shows Hawke to have embraced, first, an ethic of conviction—where he pursued ideals and denied the consequences—but then, as his career progressed, an ethic of answerability—where he appealed to responsibility to justify more pragmatic measures.[10] In the face of what Hawke saw as economic realism, political ideas were leached away altogether, along with the vitality that had made him an interesting politician.

As Stephen Mills sets it out, Hawke had a 'three-part program: an economic strategy to trade-off restraint and growth, a social plan to create national consensus, and a political ambition to achieve a sustained period of electoral dominance by the Australian Labor Party'.[11] If there was an ideal, it was to overcome the lost opportunities of the 1970s, when—under Whitlam and Fraser—the economy had foundered. There was a unifying foundation. The economic strategy involved bringing together the peak bodies of politics, business and the trade unions, achieving agreement about working together, and persuading working people of the need for sacrifice. National consensus entailed preparedness to put aside the 'them and us' divisions of the past. Labor electoral dominance meant the party's adjustment to the needs of the present, attunement to the aspirations of the people and willingness to change. The old 'Labor' issues—social justice, redistribution and welfare—were deemed to be secondary to growth, consensus and political success:

> We would love to be social democrats ticking along, making a few adjustments to the machine here and there. But we have to absolutely cut through the assumptions of the past . . . Don't judge me or my Government by whether we have blindly adhered to the standards of the past . . . Judge us by our ability to take our inherited principles and breathe new life into them, applying them anew to the task we face today.[12]

What, though, did these inherited principles amount to? 'Let me tell you what the great unchangeable goal of the ALP has been in its now nearly 100 years of existence . . . It has simply been the goal of the improvement of the lives of ordinary Australians.'[13] Combing Hawke's six hundred page *Memoirs* uncovers no aim more explicit than 'to help provide a position which will match the thoughts and aspirations of the great majority of Australian men and women, which will help weld Australians together'.[14]

These are the views of a great simplifier, the strategies of a negotiator, devoid of particular vision, or of policy specifics. The leader of *any* political party whatsoever might claim to be intent on 'improv(ing) the lives of ordinary Australians'. What is telling is the assumption that social democracy is a creed for the good times, that it involves just a few adjustments when the machine is 'ticking along'. Another history might suggest instead that social democracy has been about attempts to remake the machine! Hawke confused means with ends, and, intent on the *means* of success—growth, consensus and ALP dominance—left it to others to delineate what the *goals* of that success were to be. With no competing sense of what a good life might be (and an impoverished view of social democracy), Hawke had no defence against the insistence that the single goal of our times should be economic restructuring—that this indeed, in and of itself, would lead to 'improvement of the lives of ordinary Australians'.

Hawke's *Memoirs* provide a case study of a 1980s homo politicus—an agent of change, but one almost devoid of political imagination; an actor committed to economic progress, party reform, management and process, but with only the vaguest social ends in mind. Hawke enacted the dilemma of his times, when the urgency of economics seems to have eviscerated politics. This is not to say that there were not real economic crises to be confronted, that there was no need for economic restructuring, and that all this would not require careful management. But might even these imperatives have been addressed in terms of community values?

Hawke could persuade himself that consensus is a value, that 'improved conditions' constituted a workable goal, and that this all added up to a political philosophy. But consensus about what? If we push this we come up with a further abstraction, like 'living together'—in fact, it seemed to amount to little more than a consensus about accepting the nature of things. And how were improved conditions to be achieved? Through facilitating the improved working of the economy. Thus, his principles came together in statements like: 'our particular aim is to secure, to the maximum extent possible, shared perspectives grounded in a realistic appreciation of market conditions'. That is, a realistic appreciation of market conditions set the bounds of politics. It is not that there was no room for a politics of compassion. Hawke described himself as 'a son of the manse',[15] and some social policy issues—welfare, Aboriginal reconciliation, gender equity—could evoke an emotional response. But these were not part of the big picture, and economics was always overriding.

Hawke's harping on the means of achieving growth obscured what was happening within Australia and who was benefiting. No one could be better cast as Fukuyama's 'last man'. There was nothing left with which Hawke could challenge the liberal ideal, or the liberal state: what remained was primarily economic activity. With no utopias in prospect, idealism withered to be replaced by economic calculation. Thus Hawke's progress from the ethic of conviction to that of answerability. Hawke's history curiously parallels Fukuyama's argument—ideals and Labor traditions ran into a dead-end in 1975, and had to be replaced by economic realism. Political battle, therefore, was no longer about 'the light on the hill', but just about power and personality conflicts. And of course the great conflict was with Paul Keating.

If Hawke kept one foot in the past (always, for instance, trying to claim John Curtin's mantle[16]), Paul Keating cast off intellectual lifelines and determinedly made himself a new man. He was a professional iconoclast. He was also perhaps our first post modern leader; aware of the power of representation and of the different demands of different contexts, he would measure himself against the occasion, and produce variant selves:

. . . the me of the parliamentary chamber, or the me of this kind of conversation, or the me of the doorstop interview, or the me of the cabinet room discussion, or me . . . at home is a completely different me. I do what I do in there (Parliament) because it's the cockpit of Australian politics . . .[17]

Observers mused over the contrast between the warm, charming, somewhat shy, private man and the theatrically adept and aggressive political performer.[18] Versions of both were transmitted in the public domain: the friendly, humble, essentially family-oriented Keating chatted with Phillip Adams and Mary Kostakidis on SBS television's 'Talkshow', but the intensely self-contained, chillingly arrogant political bruiser who never dropped his guard was the Keating we saw on ABC–TV's 'Labor in Power'.[19] To the new man, the difference didn't matter: there was no advantage in presenting a unified 'me'.

Significantly, Keating saw politics in terms of particular people against whom he measured himself. Where Whitlam, for instance, was drawn to politics by the failure of Curtin's 'powers' referendum in 1944 and the sense that something had to be done,[20] Keating time and again explained his impetus in terms of great men in history:

[Roosevelt and Churchill] . . . were the two that I thought, well, if that's the business they're in, that's the business I should be in . . . They would take positions and do things and they had the sense of leadership about them where they would not always take the safe position, not do the conventional thing.[21]

While others depict his adoption of Jack Lang as philosophical mentor, Keating talks instead of being drawn to Lang 'just because he was a big doer':

[Lang] . . . gave me a sense of a round of history, and he was a very strong, huge personality, gigantic personality . . . you couldn't meet him and [not see it], all the power, huge power. He'd push the views down your throat.[22]

Keating summarised such tendencies by talking of himself as 'a star lover'[23] (and his self-description as the Placido Domingo of Australian politics invited us to identify him as among the stars), and welcomed his inclusion by an interviewer among the 'political crazies . . . those who go where others fear to tread'.[24]

Keating came from a staunch Labor family, began his political apprenticeship early, and underwent a prolonged socialisation in the Labor machine.[25] He carried ideas from that context with him. But it is as well to remember that the real impetus was this measuring of himself against great men in history, that these men represented a spectrum of views by no means congruent with Labor traditions (significantly, it was Churchill to whom he returned most persistently[26]), and that he valued not their beliefs, but their actions: they were 'big doers'. A measure of how unusual this is, again, is provided by comparing Keating's account of his political inspiration with that of Whitlam. Whitlam was another ambitious, confrontational politician (he coined the 'crash through or crash' phrase of himself), but when asked to explain his politics, always spoke of 'the program' rather than of personal ambitions.[27] Keating will speak in general terms of a program but his attention remains on the 'stars' and on the battles:

> I just hope that at the end of it, people think that I never missed an opportunity . . . that I never threw the fight anywhere . . . Integrity goes very much to this, that you don't throw the fight in the cabinet room, in the nation, in the country, in the public debate, that you don't squib them. In other words, that you see a problem and you go and try and get it resolved.[28]

The ad hocery of 'see[ing] a problem and . . . get[ting] it resolved' doesn't do justice to the changes Keating achieved, but does suggest something of the nature of his conception of the agenda—I return to this below.

One way of reading the politics of the 1980s is in terms of the way Keating (given to measuring himself against giants) measured himself against Hawke, and of how, increasingly, that process was imposed on the public debate. Nothing encapsulates this better than the documentary television series 'Labor in Power'.[29]

The testimony of ALP insiders shows that Keating managed, increasingly, to persuade others to share his assumptions, forcing Hawke to become reactive rather than the initiator. Keating's views of leadership, that it should be forceful, authoritative, prepared to confront opposition, were those by which Hawke—the negotiator, the builder of consensus—came to be judged. Perhaps the most extraordinary thing about 'Labor in Power' is that it accepts, and persuades one to accept, Keating's own estimate of his centrality. There are many manifestations of Hawke's narcissism, but 'Labor in Power' remains Keating's story—the comments of the insiders all work to this end. And the story they tell should remind us of the sorts of attributes we noted Keating himself admiring in the men on whom he modelled himself. They were, as we've seen, 'big doers', authoritative, men who (like Lang) 'would push his view down your throat', men who impressed through sheer power of personality. In just such terms have his colleagues come to see Keating:

> [Keating] was so certain of what he said. He was charming, he was humorous, he was absolutely devastating and derisory of anyone that argued against him. (Peter Cook)

> Trying to tell Paul anything has always been a difficult task. Trying to tell him he is wrong is well-nigh impossible . . . [And later] And he has an intimidating style, which he used pretty well. In cabinet he used [it] brilliantly . . . It represents a commitment to authority and the way it's exercised. [And later again] . . . For some he can bruise not just the ego, but the spirit, and that's when he goes too far. (Graham Richardson)

We might read this as Keating becoming his ideal. But in the sheer projection of willpower, self-belief translated into unquestioned belief in the idea of the moment:

> Paul is a passionate proselytiser . . . his strength is that he's such a brilliant advocate, his weakness is that his powerful convictions can lead him into error . . . [And later] Paul Keating's greatest weakness as a politician . . . the flip side of his brilliance as an advocate, [is] that he passionately believes what he is saying, no matter what it is, and that leads him into self-delusion. (Peter Walsh)

There were mistakes, but when they were recognised, it was the advisers, in Keating's view, who got it wrong: 'We were fitted up with the policies and rhetoric of the eighties. We had to change that, and change our position'. This led, though, as much to reinforcing his belief in the necessity for personal centrality as to consideration of alternative advice:

> [Treasury officers] . . . were making their best judgments, but their best judgments were not good enough . . . We all shared that mistake, but it only convinced me that what I should do as a prime minister was run much more of that policy myself. In other words, be less likely to take as given advice from the bureaucracy.

The unusualness of this response is underlined by remembering that leaders as different as Whitlam and Fraser, when facing similar problems with the bureaucracy, sought to multiply their sources of advice: only Keating has seen the option as 'run[ning] more of that policy myself'.

The repeated trope of solitary endeavour, keeping the show on the road by his own efforts, while in contrast 'Bob's a very lucky guy, he always ends up with a group of people who'll look after him when he's in strife', testifies to Keating's image of himself as owing nothing to anybody. But his are the gifts of hardball politics—of confrontation, strategy, winning at all costs—rather than of building the connections integral to the political imagination. The Labor Party swapped negotiation for a leadership solipsism, masquerading as authority. Yet so protean did Keating prove to be that he could start remaking himself after 1992.

What did all this mean for the ideational basis of politics, and for the imagination behind it? The fact that Keating was, indeed, 'crazy', prepared to go over the top, an audacious performer, a man with considerable facility with language, made him just the sort of 'star' who preoccupied the press gallery, and, increasingly, the intelligentsia generally. What they failed to notice was that the show was always much more about Keating's imagination of himself as 'a big doer' than about ideas. The inadequacy was made more difficult to detect because Keating was, at one level, very good with ideas, extraordinarily quick with new scripts. In the 1980s, he was the perfect spokesman for the new agenda. So expert did he become that the seamless performance dazzled the media (all of whom were advocates of the new orthodoxy anyway), mystified the electorate (to whom the jargon was unintelligible) and precluded real political questions arising at all—since everything was reinterpreted in terms of economics.

In policy terms, Keating's domination in the 1980s represented abandonment to the Treasury: as former Treasury official and banker, David Morgan remarked:

> Treasury always had its own agenda. It got more of its agenda up in the decade of the Hawke/Keating Government than for the rest of the postwar period combined.[30]

The Treasury line[31] depended on arcane models of how the world works, models that were difficult to make intelligible in everyday political exchange, and which, in any case, were not up for debate (this is simply how the world is). Hence, there was a sea-change in political language: a shift from the rhetoric of persuasion to the rhetoric of prescription. It was inevitable that Keating would be the one to confront us most forcefully with the insistence that politics was no longer about listening to the community, but about confronting it with the inevitable—his most famous prescription being 'the recession we had to have'.

Keating's purposes matched Hawke's agenda (only their ambitions were in conflict) and for most of the 1980s it was he who pedalled the one big idea—not a political idea at all—that the market was the answer. Yet his facility with scripts meant an ability to adapt, and in 1992, in response to new pressures, the script began to change. But the move away from market solutions was tentative, it had little impact on the 1993 election (which was fought on the politics of fear rather than new ideas), and only when the election was won did Keating voice the new script with any earnestness. Then it was to show how thoroughly political ideas had been diluted.

Keating's address to 'the true believers' on election night, 13 March 1993, professed a renewed faith in collective values:

This is a victory for the true believers, the people who in hard times have kept the faith and to the Australian people going through hard times—it makes their act of faith all that much greater . . .

. . . the Liberal Party wanted to change Australia from the place it has become, a cooperative, decent, nice place to live where people have regard for one another . . . we have turned the corner. The growth is coming through. We will see ourselves as a sophisticated trading country in Asia . . . It offers tremendous opportunities for Australians and now we have to do it and we have to do it compassionately . . . we'll care about those people out there, particularly the unemployed . . . If we can't get them back to work immediately . . . we are not going to leave them in the lurch and we are going to put our hand out and we are going to pull them up behind us . . . (we'll) get this country of opportunity off and running, but keeping the opportunity for everybody . . . keeping those great nostrums of access and equity. Getting people into the game. The policies of inclusion . . . [32]

John Murphy has shown how nostalgic and archaic was Keating's appeal to 'the true believers': it ignored both huge changes in his party's base, and the way in which the economic and policy changes he had wrought brought disintegration to the communities that might once have been addressed in such terms.[33]

In 1994, however, 'policies of inclusion' began to be addressed, and Keating's reinvention of himself as a socially concerned leader—initiated with One Nation, and expressed in the 'True Believers' speech—came to flower. The process was evident in a series of headlining policy initiatives. The Working Nation jobs compact was designed to specify how the disadvantaged are to be 'pulled up behind us'. The Creative Nation package was intended to resuscitate the arts and national identity. The promotion of Aboriginal reconciliation in concert with native title legislation as a response to the High Court's Mabo decision was of great importance. The appointment of a 'civics expert group' to revive responsible citizen politics and the institution of a 'national strategies conference' were also part of this steering of policies.[34] Alongside, there were contributions to the debate about an Australian republic, the achievement of gender equity, and the promotion of health and welfare.[35] There was also an insistence on the importance of ideas.[36]

This was a prolific agenda. Much within it was innovative, responsive to the changed world, and potentially productive. How, then, can I continue to argue that Keating's approach, even then, signified a failure of political imagination? In part, I must concede ground: he responded cleverly to what he described as having been 'fitted up with the policies and rhetoric of the eighties', and it's hard to think of another politician who might have attempted this. I also concede that he provided an opening for the revival of political imagination. But the way his agenda was put together shows both the advantages, and the limits, of his facility with new scripts.

The advantages were these. Keating adopted new ideas with conviction (though remember Walsh's remark that he always 'passionately believes what he is saying'), and this made him a persuasive advocate. He was thus able to form alliances with interested parties on important issues (and Labor's ability to create coalitions of interest groups was crucial to its unexpected success in the 1993 federal election[37]). He was able to sustain the theatre of conviction politics to mobilise change. He was unfazed by contradictions with earlier messages; able to slough off the past 'self' in favour of a new project. Yet his 1996 electoral defeat showed his failure to persuade the public generally of the significance of these new directions.

The chief disadvantage was that there was no grand rhetorical scheme, which is to say no comprehensive social vision, behind it all. We were not told how these schemes connected with our everyday problems. There was no attempt to explain the linkages *between* these lofty plans to the community (let alone to consult with it beforehand). Thus, they contributed little to an enhanced sense of certainty about where the country was heading. It was as if a world view could be built up piecemeal through discrete policy initiatives—each of which was sold as the great breakthrough. If you look back at Fraser, or Whitlam, or Menzies,[38] you find that their statements of what they want the world to be are spelt out separately from policy—policy *follows on* from a detailed idealisation of a social world. Menzies' 'forgotten people' speech, for instance, incorporates a precise and detailed picture of how people should live; of the relations between individual, state and society; of gender relations and the influence of women; of the necessity to constrain elites—and a set of moral evaluations to boot. The point is not to endorse Menzies' view (his is not a world I'd want to go back to), but to say that, for all the brilliance of discrete policy initiatives, Keating's ideal did not seem to have progressed from such abstract generalisations as that Australia should be 'inclusive, kind, gentle . . . [a] nice place'.[39]

Each new social policy initiative seemed a one-off. I like Donald Horne's description of this:

> . . . Keating's erratic genius is that he comes out now and
> again with his spray can and sketches a big, bright picture
> that stays on the wall as a new part of the political scene . . .
> It's as if 'the economy', or 'the Republic', or 'Asia', and now
> 'the arts', did not exist before the historic moment when, out
> of the void, they were one by one created by Mr Keating.[40]

But, Horne goes on to say, there's a sort of cultural blindness behind it. And this lack of an integrating imagination has its effects on those policies.

The pronouncements flowing from *One Nation* each replicated the pattern of the 'true believers' speech: a recognition that not only economic restructuring but also social problems needed to be addressed; a grand, bright picture of a possible innovation (Keating's 'spray can'); but then an inability to mobilise any rhetoric to bring these fragments together other than that of economic reform.

One Nation[41] forecast increased infrastructure spending, some targeted assistance programs and a cautiously framed industry policy, and was instantly condemned by economic commentators for this profligacy.[42] But it still concentrated above all on a low tax, smaller public sector agenda, with further deregulation and enhanced economic integration in Asia as the way ahead.[43] It implied some criticism of the private sector, and greater willingness to consider limited market intervention, but it reiterated the general commitment to free market orthodoxy and was notably deficient in its ability to depict a fairer society.

The *Working Nation* package, on which so much in the way of social justice was to hang, was essentially a job training and work readiness package. For all its innovative attempts to break down the divisions between work and welfare, to provide job support and reskilling of the workforce, it functioned entirely within the bounds of the economic 'realities' established as orthodoxy in the 1980s. The point is clear if you compare it with the landmark *White Paper on Full Employment* of 1945. In the 1940s, the approach was to think about how the economy should be structured to ensure full employment (that is, economic management was subject to a political vision). In the 1990s, politics was secondary, economic structures were taken as given and we had to work within the terms they dictated. So what *Working Nation* proposed were palliative measures. It is important that, at the very least, we take such palliative measures. But might there not have been a more comprehensive political vision? Many would join Keating in saying that is not possible—it would go beyond the disciplines demanded by the global market—but other options, as Langmore and Quiggin,[44] for instance, suggest, are thinkable (see chapter 6).

The *Creative Nation* policy pronouncement contained much to gladden arts professionals and the culture industries. The link between support for the arts and economic prosperity was evident. The forward-looking embrace of the new technologies that comprise the information superhighway was notable. But there was a strong indication that technology would dictate our options (rather than citizen choice). And the document was curiously thin on what the place of cultural activity is (and should be) in our everyday lives. ' . . . [T]he document abandons discussion of community engagement in cultural life. Members of the community are now transformed from engaged citizens into "arts consumers". (Not even arts *users*).'[45] That *Creative Nation* touted our ability to sell our culture to the countries of our region as a benefit of cultural revival, yet was unclear about the community this revival was to serve, showed how far we were from fully recovering the social dimension.

What of Keating's imaginative initiatives on such matters as republicanism, and Aboriginal rights (especially in legislation relating to the High Court's *Mabo* decision)? Independent national identity and black–white reconciliation were important issues but they did not originate with Keating, and were deployed for other ends as much as for their intrinsic importance. They were emblematic causes, one of them encouraging commitment to a new version of Australia, and the other elevating a pressing matter of social justice, without ever addressing the specifics of the post-republican community or the structural and economic impediments to more general social justice. Like the other initiatives, they lacked the lineaments of a bigger picture. They were in the nature of a *selective* commitment to alternatives to the market, but did not in themselves provide the script with which the economic orthodoxy of the 1980s could be contested.

In fact, these many cultural and social strands for Keating always related back to a picture not of what society should be like, but of where he wanted Australia to be in the world: at the top table; productively integrated with Asia; speaking 'the languages of our neighbours'; a 'familiar and valued part of the commercial landscape of the Asia–Pacific'; in which 'our national identity is clearer to us and our neighbours . . . our national culture is shaped by, and helps to shape, the cultures around us'.[46]

Domestically, the Hilmer reforms[47] held sway. By 1994, as an outcome of a Commonwealth Heads of Government meeting, it was being argued that a better future was to be achieved through national uniform competition legislation— with federal and State agreement to allow the carve-up of monopolies in markets including gas, electricity and railways and competition in the professions. Freeing up the national economy was still the singular answer. That no distinction was made between public utilities and professions indicated that little thought had been given to areas where public sector involvement might be fruitful and those where the market is enough. Certainly the dysfunctional effects of British experiments in 'carving up monopolies' in electricity and transport (see chapter 4) were ignored.

The governing impulse here remains economic progress. The great cultural initiatives were introduced with much fanfare, and then Keating moved on. Or rather, he moved back, continually to insist on the importance of competition policy, or, above all, of APEC.[48] These, it seemed, were the persisting templates against which other achievements were to be measured. Keating continually failed to imagine himself in the shoes of that growing group of those pinched hard by economic reform: what did APEC, or cultural exports, or reconciliation have to do with their efforts to make ends meet? So Keating, for all his passion, failed to achieve the social democracy at which he aimed. And, as economic trends turned sour again in 1995, he had no integrating vision with which to defend against the financial markets' demands for 'more discipline', no persuasive rejoinder to the opposition's claim that we'd been allowed 'five minutes of sunlight', and then the sky fell in again. Perhaps his difficulty was that he had done as much as anyone in public life to bring about the realisation of Fukuyama's forecast: a time when philosophy and political imagination were defeated by the sense of the inevitable, the sense that there could not be anything fundamentally new to say.[49]

No way back? Liberal leaders in the wilderness

Malcolm Fraser may have been the last voice of ameliorative liberalism as Liberal Party leader. In the 1980s, there were still appeals to social conscience by some in the Liberal Party, such as Chris Puplick and Ian McPhee, but the fashion was to deem Fraser wrong, and to emphasise an ever more individualistic philosophy. Fraser's successor, Andrew Peacock, was not the man to breathe new life into Liberal philosophy in opposition.

John Howard, who beat Peacock in a leadership challenge, gave more attention to ideas, as his 1988 manifesto *Future Directions*[50] indicated. In this he attempted to pair the economic orthodoxies of the day with a social conservatism recognising community anxieties about change and turmoil. But his was a limited project, relying on a nostalgic evocation of the virtues of the past, and a claim that 'traditional' family values were central to Liberalism. It did not persuasively connect with contemporary problems.

In any case, it was not enough to save his leadership: that had been weakened by the 'Joh for Canberra' campaign in 1987, when the populist Queensland premier managed to fragment the conservative alliances that offered the only hope of defeating Labor. Bad judgment in a debate about immigration in 1988—when Howard inadvertently raised fears of racial discrimination but then, in the interests of demonstrating strong leadership, refused to change tack—was the last straw. Howard lost his chance, and he was sidelined by the return of Peacock as leader in 1989 as another election approached.

In the 1990 election campaign, Peacock acted like someone schooled in an artificial notion of how leaders should look and perform rather than acting from conviction. He was bombastic and self-righteous, and one was always uneasily aware of the performance—it was always 'mock indignation' on display. In contrast, his deputy, John Hewson, though relatively new, showed the energy and acumen to appear an effective workhorse. When Labor won again, it was no surprise that Hewson replaced Peacock as Liberal leader.

Hewson—who had combined careers as academic economist, political adviser, financial market consultant and bank director—presented himself as someone who knew the 'real world' (meaning economics and business) rather than as a professional politician. He represented the Liberal Party's complete commitment to free market economics, and a decisive repudiation of the ameliorative liberalism championed by former leaders from Menzies to Fraser. Where Keating merely articulated the one big idea of the day, Hewson was defined by it—and believed in nothing else. He did not believe in the Liberal traditions (and explicitly cast aside the Menzies inheritance). He was too busy to indulge in internal party politicking. He had no judgment for people and no taste for compromise or deals. He was a fighter and a doer who set goals and pursued them relentlessly. His major goal was the plan encapsulated in *Fightback!* The way in which he pursued the plan was self-defeating. And nothing could reveal more clearly that—taken to its logical extreme—the free market conviction entails the abandonment of politics.

Hewson's agenda became explicit with the release of *Fightback!*[51] in November 1991. This lengthy policy document turned its back on the tentative rethinking of social vision evident in Howard's *Future Directions*. Indeed, it seemed to abandon the tenets of ameliorative liberalism developed by philanthropic capitalists since the 1860s, as Hugh Emy has pointed out.[52] It aimed to push the free market reform process further and faster by directly confronting the interests allegedly benefiting from the interventionist state. Hawke's negotiation and consensus building were seen as giving too much ground to those interests. As a political strategy, it depended wholly on electors (as individuals) recognising that better conditions would be achieved when they were 'freed' to help themselves.

Fightback! promised reductions in direct taxation—an incentive, it was said, for individuals to work harder. These reductions were to be funded by a 15 per cent tax on goods and services (GST)—not an infringement on individual discretion, so the argument ran, since it was a tax at the point of consumption. The GST would most benefit those on higher incomes (who had most to gain from reduced personal taxation), and did not promise more discretion to the less advantaged whose conditions of work were beyond their control and whose consumption choices were largely dictated by necessities (rent, food, clothing). It was a regressive measure, and it was the ALP's ability to capitalise on fear of taxes that was ruinous to the Liberal campaign.

Along with tax changes, *Fightback!* promised impositions against 'big government': reductions and redirections in federal spending; a much wider program of privatisation with proceeds from the sale of public sector assets to reduce government debt; a national savings strategy; reduced funding to the States; much more stringent targeting (and some privatisation) of welfare programs. Faith in the market, and a model of individual self-help were central:

> The whole purpose of this great reform package is to give individual Australians the chance to fightback for a better life. This reform package will put Government in its place and put Australians back in control of their own lives . . . The whole thrust of our policy is to strengthen the individual against the state—in particular to strengthen the forgotten people, the low and middle income earners, against the forces which control and limit their lives.[53]

The self-conscious reference to 'the forgotten people' is intended to resurrect Menzies, but Liberal policy makers had forgotten that Menzies positioned these people *between* the millstones of state bureaucracies on one side and economically privileged elites on the other. The *Fightback!* rhetoric hung on the opposition between individual and state, with individual choice thought to be most fully exercised in the market, and the market efficiently distributing benefits in response to individual choices.

> The Liberals appeared to take no account of the practical experience with markets—or the intellectual reaction to laissez-faire—since about the middle of the nineteenth century. In particular, they seemed indifferent to the many criticisms and warnings . . . concerning the adverse—and sometimes disastrous—impact of completely free markets upon the fabric of society . . . one sensed a formidable ignorance . . . about the internal complexities of liberal democratic societies and the actual balance of forces within Australian society . . . how far could one support a program whose progenitors seemed so unaware of the passage of social and intellectual history since about 1860—including, especially, the history of liberalism itself?[54]

Fightback! 'showed too little regard for mounting social inequalities', and 'left the success of structural reform wholly to the rationality of market forces, in effect placing its faith in the profit motive'.[55] It was unlikely that people already anxious about the pace of change would be won by this strategy. Indeed, when adverse public responses began to register, there was some modification with the release of *Fightback Mark* 2.

These modifications included removing the GST on basic food-stuffs, postponing some tax cuts, offering greater infrastructure expenditure—piecemeal concessions that under-mined Hewson's claim to a coherent package representing special expertise. Nonetheless, it was Hewson's manifesto both against the Liberal past, and the blunders of Labor in the present, and in its essentials he could not let it go.

The best account of what this meant in terms of Liberal political thought is given by Judith Brett. She has argued that the form of individualism promoted by the contemporary Liberal Party is at odds with individualism as understood by the party in the past, is increasingly disconnected from com-monsense experience, and—most importantly in terms of political imagination—leaves it unable to find a convincing contemporary language of national unity.[56]

Individualism in the eyes of the party's founders was associated with independence and self-reliance. This sat easily alongside a solidary language of social responsibility, service and obligation—and a pairing of rights with duties. The con-temporary shift to the language of choice and freedom has displaced independence. The expansion of individual choice has been the central legitimating idea for consumerism. But this is a language that does not fit with the once integrating language of duty and obligation. 'A political party which makes the language of freedom of individual choice a central symbol today has a daunting task to develop a convincing language of social unity; its individualism is as likely to evoke fears of social breakdown as market mechanisms reject those unable to compete, as it is to evoke the social whole.'[57] A language once well-suited to describing the new experience of private affluence (and the duties that went with it) after the war has been displaced by possessive individualism.

Yet the post-war experience has also encouraged people more readily to see themselves as at least partly socially-formed. Sociological understandings have permeated commonsense, and explanations of inequity that commence with the assertion that 'we are all individuals' do not coincide with our commonsense understandings of the way social structures and expectations constrain life chances. The Liberal

Party, argues Brett, never did overcome the 'fundamental difficulties in the relationship between its underlying social philosophy and the commonsense understandings of contemporary Australia'.[58] The market could not provide a rhetoric of social unity.

A further problem was that Hewson was an evangelist. He knew he was right, so had nothing to learn—from the party, from the grassroots, from the past, from the community. Campaign footage in 1993 showed him apparently incapable of listening, merely waiting with an intense look for others to stop talking so that he could give them 'the answer'. His plans for reform were bold and radical—but they were almost entirely concerned with economics and left community concerns and social issues in the margins. Howard's attempt to marry social principle with free market economics in *Future Directions* was entirely forgotten. Eventually Hewson suffered the fate of all those incapable of listening to others: with no projection of flexibility, responsiveness, or the chance of dialogue, he became increasingly difficult to listen to. It hardly seemed to matter: convinced not only of his plan but also that the Labor government was doomed, he simply confronted those interests who might stand in the way of his reforms—though many of them (e.g. manufacturing industry) might be thought to have been Liberal supporters.

In the end, Hewson induced sufficient fear in the electorate of the sort of change he envisaged to turn the 'unlosable' election around. He had a vision of the market, but no sense of the community: it is not surprising, then, that he was 'unable to explain simply to the people the practical and social aspects of his economic program so they understood the sort of Australia he wanted'.[59] It is unlikely that he had any very clear view of what the social and cultural aspects of his program were likely to be.

With the 1993 election defeat came the recognition that Hewson and his party were adrift, with no lifeline to the past, and with the future they had imagined repudiated. Hewson had been represented as bringing conviction, ideas, even academic credibility, to a party that had spent too much of the 1980s bickering over Peacock and Howard, and uncertain of how to commit to the new orthodoxies while presenting an alternative to Labor. The certainties he had represented, however, led to a blind drop. Hewson clung to power—for a time it seemed there was no alternative, though internal party squabbles were unremitting.

A manifestation of how desperately attenuated the party's capacity to rethink a Liberal politics had become was the emergence of then Senator Bronwyn Bishop for a time as leadership contender. Her sole recommendations were an extraordinary capacity for self-promotion, boundless ambition, and increasing support in the polls—fuelled by incessant media exposure. But her ascendance seemed to indicate the abandonment of any ideas at all. Her populism and extreme individualism were at odds with most of the Liberal Party's history (though not, perhaps, with Hewson); their translation into policy promised disastrous consequences of the sort then being adumbrated by conservative thinkers such as John Gray and Ferdinand Mount.[60] The flirtation with Bishop represented a denial of the intellectual work that will be necessary to forge a politics appropriate to our times. Fortunately, her political limitations became starkly evident as she undertook the process of positioning herself to make a leadership bid. She undermined her own credibility, and we were saved the Bishop option.

Hewson, however, could not recover. He abandoned *Fightback!*, but he could never thereafter make clear what he stood for. A senior colleague, Peter Reith, disputed that *Fightback!* should be discarded, and some complained that Hewson had not consulted before announcing the new direction. Chaos led to active destabilisation (including the leaking of internal party polls damaging to Hewson) and open canvassing of alternative leaders. Senior party figures—eventually including party President, Tony Staley—spoke for change. As opinion firmed on the likely candidature of Alexander Downer and Peter Costello, Hewson attempted a pre-emptive strike, calling a spill of leadership positions and challenging his detractors to 'put up or shut up'. His rivals proved more organised than he had imagined: Downer and Costello, rather than individually challenging, announced a joint ticket with Downer for leader and Costello for deputy. Dubbed the 'dream team', they were described by party figures (and by a large part of the media) as representing a 'generational change'. In May 1994, Downer and Costello defeated Hewson and his deputy (Michael Wooldridge) in the ballot Hewson had called.

Great hopes were invested in Downer and Costello. They rode high in the polls, and enjoyed a prolonged honeymoon in media and electorate opinion. But, significantly, the leadership change had been made with no reference to policy priorities. Instead, it was claimed that these were 'professionals' who could turn the party around.

Alexander Downer was the son of one of the founders of the modern Liberal Party, former MP, Menzies cabinet member and diplomat, the late Sir Alexander Downer. Much was made of this heritage, and Downer himself claimed, 'I am born of the Liberal Party and I am a creature of the Liberal Party'.[61] Few noticed that his descriptions of his 'progressive conservative' views showed no understanding of either liberal or conservative traditions—he worked with labels rather than ideas. His attractions were said to be that he was 'deft', 'pragmatic', 'self-confident', 'no novice'.[62] He had shown himself competent and focused within the discipline of shadow portfolios. Peter Costello had made an early mark in student politics, and then as an aggressive lawyer defending employer group interests. He, like Downer, had entered politics early. He'd been closely associated with hardline economic rationalism, but that was now downplayed and his skills as an effective operator were stressed. A speech on 'the four fundamentals of the Liberal way' showed Costello quite unable to link abstract ideas with ways of living in the manner predecessors like Menzies and Fraser had managed: (' . . . we believe,' said Costello, in 'the spirit of initiative . . . the spirit of humanity . . . the spirit of civic virtue . . . (and) restoration of . . . national pride in Australian decision-making, by Australians accountable to the Australian electorate.').[63] Who might not have said this? There's nothing about it distinctive to the Liberal Party (or any other) and its implications for policy, or programs, or values, are not evident. Nonetheless, as a shrewd operator and a confrontational politician, Costello had a formidable reputation.

The dream did not last. Partly it was because, without the discipline of a portfolio framework, Downer's judgment proved erratic and politically counterproductive. But, surely, it was also because there was no imagination—having won the leadership, the 'dream team' had no dream, no idea what to do with the opportunity. The sole aim was to regain government. There were only the most confused statements of what they would govern *for*. It was said that hardline ideology had been jettisoned, and that economics must be leavened with social concerns, but Downer's shadow ministry had economic dries in the most senior portfolios. The initial 'battle plan' depended on slogans. The coalition, said Downer, would fight on family policy, foreign debt, unemployment and pride in national symbols—and the assertion that 'it is time we put the dark vitriolic years of Labor in power behind us'.[64] There was a concern to provide only statements of directions that 'would not provide the ALP with the sort of target it had in *Fightback!*'. A recurrent promise to issue a blueprint on coalition policy directions was dragged out from May to September, and there were concerted attempts to dampen expectations before it was issued—it was to provide not policy but policy foundations. The resulting document, *The Things that Matter*, was shaped by polling, to reflect what people wanted. It emphasised 'the family', job creation, community empowerment and Australian patriotism, but was torn between giving enough specifics to provide a sense of direction, and avoiding the detail that would provide the government with a target (especially a target that could be costed).

Broad populist themes without policy detail were not enough. The tactic encouraged questions about whether this leadership team had anything to say on the issues troubling contemporary Australia. It allowed scope for Keating to label Downer a 'policy flake' and his party a 'policy free zone'—and he relentlessly turned up the pressure of this attack, to devastating effect. But above all, it fostered a sense that these leaders had no firm guidelines, and would say whatever they thought an audience wanted to hear: there was no constraint on their judgment. And, increasingly, Downer's judgment was seen to be awry.

A spectacularly public series of unforced errors undermined Downer. His electoral honeymoon came to an abrupt end when he stumbled badly over coalition Aboriginal policy. In mid-July he showed himself unclear on its detail in a radio interview; in late July he told a West Australian Liberal audience that the Coalition might repeal native title legislation; within days he not only softened his *Mabo* stance, but also told Aboriginal communities he would agree to continue an Aboriginal veto over mining, in contradiction of coalition policy; and—challenged to explain the contradictions—he gave confused replies, and the disingenuous defence of being carried away by emotion. His poll standing slumped by record levels. Barely a month later, and within three days of launching his vaunted directions statement, he lampooned its title with a bad joke—suggesting, in view of its dealing with domestic violence, it might be called 'The Things that Batter'—which generated such outrage and ridicule that the whole exercise was effectively abandoned—and still the gaffes continued. He needlessly antagonised ethnic communities by threatening to 'deny them access' if they criticised the coalition stance on racial vilification legislation. He attacked the so-called 'Canberra establishment' when his whole life had been led as a Canberra civil servant and a career politician. His attempt to capitalise on the government's disquiet over Sydney aircraft noise would have entailed a substantial reduction in operating capacity for the busiest airport in the country. He courted the moderates, but (by inattention or intent) allowed the attempt by leading moderate, Robert Hill to translate from the Senate to the House, to be subverted. After a period of public jousting, he sacked Hewson from his frontbench, but as his own position slid away, approached him about a possible return—only to have Hewson publicly offer to return on condition that he be appointed in Costello's place as shadow treasurer (and Hewson's provocative announcement was the first Downer's frontbench colleagues knew of these discussions). His attempts to assert authority through party modernisation to give the executive greater control had only qualified support. The issues on which he tried to move the party to the middle ground—on the republic, on sexual privacy legislation and on racial hatred legislation—were all responses to ALP initiatives: this was once more the party of reaction and thus unwittingly Downer played to Keating's agenda. Even when he achieved a victory of sorts (for instance, in his handling of the party's conference), he made no dent on his crash in the polls—which by year's end translated into the longest sustained slump ever recorded for an opposition leader.

That he could not regain the confidence of colleagues became evident. Critical internal party documents were leaked (including party commissioned polls adverse to Downer). Tactics like those which had destroyed Hewson came into play. A campaign of destabilisation by disaffected elements within the party dominated the news, undermining efforts to set a distinct policy agenda. Downer vowed that he 'would not be spooked' and would fight to the end, but after only eight months, his leadership was terminally damaged. It was a measure of Costello's skill that he managed to maintain loyalty as deputy leader and to ride out Downer's demise without damage to his reputation. Indeed, his prospects of succeeding Downer were again canvassed. But the person shadowing Downer, and to whom the party finally turned—not without reluctance in some quarters—was John Howard.

Howard achieved a renaissance that even he had thought impossible: 'I accept,' he had said after Downer's election, 'that I'll never be the leader of the Liberal Party again. It's out of the question'.[65] He had, however, projected a moderate image, describing himself as a 'tolerant conservative' as opposed to the radical conservatism he'd previously claimed as leader. He distanced himself from his 'mistaken' remarks on Asian immigration of 1988. He backed away from the big-bang economically oriented approach to policy. As Downer's position deteriorated, Howard was mentioned more and more frequently as the credible alternative and in November he indicated that he was 'available'. He would not challenge, it was said, but would only accept a draft. By December 1994, however, Howard's allies were organising the numbers for him. In January 1995, when it was clear that he had the numbers to win, Howard confronted Downer and persuaded him that his position was untenable. Downer agreed to step aside, and on 30 January 1995, Howard was re-elected unopposed as Liberal leader (with Costello continuing as his deputy). What were his attractions?

The sheer depth of his experience of and commitment to the Liberal Party ranked highly. While Downer claimed he was 'born of the party' (and showed decisively that this was not enough!), Howard was that rarer creature on the conservative side—one who had been schooled in the machine. He had joined the party at seventeen, became president of the Young Liberals at twenty-three, served on the New South Wales state executive for eleven years before being elected to parliament, and, by 1995, had been an MP for twenty-one years.[66] Of course, he carried with him the baggage of an earlier leadership defeat. Whether he had learned better management and personal interaction skills remained to be proved—these had dogged his earlier incumbency. But he had persuaded enough people that he had moderated his position to be credible once more.

Against the impression that he had not been a strong enough leader last time, Howard had established an image over intervening years as the party's toughest and most effective parliamentary performer. In a context where the party, under Downer, had appeared unsure what it believed in, Howard was a politician of conviction. This was both a strength, and potentially a problem: as Rod Cameron observed:

> The party (has been) so poll-driven, and such a reflection of
> middle-class values . . . that it does not ring true . . . The
> thing that has stamped Howard as a leader of some substance
> in the past has been his conviction. The things he stood for.
> The electorate will now have to judge how his attempts to
> take the lead from his saddlebags on all the contentious issues
> sits with a man of genuine principle and conviction.[67]

Howard's initial strategy in managing this divide was to separate matters of detail (all those things on which he'd shifted ground) from the fundamentals in which, he said, he'd always believed:

> . . . certain things are enduring about my vision for Australia
> . . . I have always believed in an Australia built on reward for
> individual effort . . . I have always believed in a safety net for
> those among us who don't make it. I have always believed in
> the family as the stabilising and cohering unit of our society
> and . . . an Australia drawn from people from the four
> corners of the Earth, but uniting together behind a common
> set of Australian values.[68]

Again, these are generalisations without clear links to a policy agenda. Howard, however, maintained party discipline, and people were evidently prepared to accept his 'fundamentals' and to take the details on trust. Howard signalled that his would be a softer, inclusive liberalism. Even in his radical conservative phase, he had genuinely attempted to leaven economics with social concerns in *Future Directions*—the last Liberal attempt to do so. His limit was that he persisted in seeing the family as the core of social policy. This could be a winning strategy, as the 1994 Republican campaign in the US showed. It won in Australia in 1996. But it was a limited platform from which to re-imagine solutions to the collective problems of social justice, equity, fair life chances for all. It offered little ground for reviving civil society (see chapter 7) and the strong likelihood—in the absence of more comprehensive philosophical principles—that all will be subsumed again by the supposed imperatives of economic management.

The sorry history of the period from 1993 to 1995 showed how much the Liberal organisation had withered, how much politics itself had been forgotten, in the belief in leaders, and in one big idea. There were no resources to draw on in the reformulation of policy. When the party's headquarters were refurbished, Gerard Henderson was quick to note that more thought had gone into catering facilities than into a library.[69] The marginalisation of moderates meant there was not the diversity to generate lively debate *within* the party. Former participants had to express their criticisms from outside, in newspapers (Ian MacPhee, for instance) and books (Chris Puplick, for instance). The dark side of the individualism so pervasive in the party was that it had no collective way of dealing with the leaders, in whom all hope lay. When they failed, they were left hanging on the wire, without effective institutional support, while those whose hopes had been disappointed covertly joined the media to advance a public process of destabilisation and humiliation (witness the destruction of Hewson and Downer). Laura Tingle summed up the Downer case:

> Downer did not single-handedly destroy his leadership. It was his own mistakes, in combination with appalling political advice, a disruptive and incompetent party machine and structure, and the endemic mischief-making of members of the parliamentary party.[70]

Howard's ascension to the leadership in 1995 did not solve any of these problems. Nor did his federal election victory in 1996 mean a philosophical recovery from the *Fightback!* debacle so much as a strategic recovery. The Coalition's intentions were obscured by Howard's refusal to release policies until the eve of the election campaign. These were oriented to specific grievances and particular anxieties, but there was no comprehensive platform. To Keating, Howard offered no target. To the people, he promised that he would govern for all and create a society in which there are opportunities for all. It was a promise attuned to the political climate: Australians wanted an end to the pain of economic and social reform, an end to Keating's assurance that if we hung on a little longer, everything would improve. It was the promise that won Howard the election. Yet it was a promise that contained inherent conflicts between what the markets will demand (continued microeconomic reform) and what the people now expect, and between Howard's individualism and the sort of managed capitalism that can be the only barrier between the electorate and the harsh impacts of the global economy (see chapter 6).

An exit from this quandary, in Howard's case, could only be managed by a recovery of the philosophy of ameliorative liberalism. Ameliorative liberalism, as we have seen, is not alien to the Liberal Party: it was a fundamental tenet from Deakin through to Menzies, and Fraser continues to speak in such terms. Yet it has become desperately unfashionable (see chapters 3 and 4), and is opposed to Howard's conviction that individuals and families can solve most problems if given the 'freedom' to do so.

Well, they can't, and we know they can't. The electorate's recognition of this underlay its uneasiness with Hewson. Keating's awareness of this underlay his 1993 claim that we must reach out to those who have been disadvantaged by economic reform, and pull them up behind us. His failure convincingly to achieve this contributed to his defeat.

Howard, refusing to see the paradox between his belief and his policies, tailored his campaign to this mood. We accepted his professions on faith, gambling on the promise of a comfort Keating had been unable to deliver. Yet only a comprehensive rethinking of ameliorative liberalism in today's context could provide the framework to transform Howard's piecemeal policies into an integrated program, capable of further development. Only such an integrated program might deliver on Howard's promise to the electorate.

At the time of writing, Howard faced three high-risk options. To battle on with the incompatible demands of both further 'market' freedom and social responsibility, and account for failure as the unfortunate consequence of Labor's 'mismanagement'. To concede that what he promised in 1996 is not achievable if the demands of 'the economy' (as these are conventionally understood in Australia) are to be met, and try to persuade the electorate that further pain and even more disparity between the rich and the poor is inevitable. (This, given the volatility of the electorate, might destroy his government.) Or to take on the biggest challenge of all—revising the conventions of economic orthodoxy, confronting his own tenacious individualism, and recovering the strand of ameliorative liberalism that the electorate demands and which might make his party relevant to the next century. This would be a Liberal renaissance indeed, a recovery of political imagination such as Keating only groped towards. But given the recent history of the Liberal Party, and Howard's refusal to recognise the inherent conflict in his position, it seems a most unlikely outcome unless the sorts of arguments canvassed in this book become matters of wide debate and public pressure (see chapters 6 and 7).

The attractions of economic orthodoxy and the betrayal of the intelligentsia

Why was it possible for economics so fully to overwhelm politics in our public life? My own sense of what has happened runs like this. In the 1970s, politicians in all the market capitalist societies (but especially in the settler societies like Australia whose economies were already highly dependent on world markets) confronted the effects of high modernity without understanding its causes. People experienced an almost intolerable increase in the pace of change, with the ability of transnational business and finance to generate movements of capital, resources and peoples across national boundaries without regard for intranational sensibilities. Political leaders saw the effects of the rapid circulation of capital eroding the ability of the state to control the nation's affairs. What they understood to be happening was that state agencies themselves were failing: *this* was the 'crisis of the state'. The people expected political remedies for their dislocation, economic uncertainty and suffering: the politicians became convinced that the old solutions no longer worked (which is the force of Kelly's 'end of certainty'). In this context, economic rationalism flourished, because it fulfilled three essential purposes. It explained that dislocation was an after-effect of the old order, the price that had to be paid for inappropriate state activities. It justified the processes of internationalisation. And it allowed politicians to disclaim responsibility for what happened: it was a rationale for divestiture of state responsibilities ('the market' would solve what politicians had been unable to).

Once committed to this techno-specialism, politicians became more and more prey to their advisers, and less reliant on their parties, the grassroots, or the community, none of whom could be expected to understand 'the economy'. Often, by eliding market and society, they lost the ability to conceptualise the community: as Hewson graphically showed in 1993, they lost the sense of who to address, or how.

By the mid-1980s, George Orwell's pessimistic fable from 1948 of an authoritarian future, *1984*, seemed misconceived. Liberal values and 'free' economies had triumphed, and the authoritarian communist regimes were in their last days. But this little book is not just an expression of 1940s despair. It is, centrally, a fable about language. In particular, it is about a form of language and a habit of thought that made alternative views—and hence political action—impossible. Orwell shaped his conceit around a fabricated language, 'Newspeak', and a controlling bureaucratic agency, the 'Ministry of Truth'. It reminds me, however, that the various attempts to proclaim 'the end of ideology', Daniel Bell's in the 1950s as much as Francis Fukuyama's in the 1990s, have had as their avowed aim that ideas other than their preferred one of individualistic liberalism will become, literally, unthinkable. The agency in their scheme is history, not bureaucratic fiat, and the means are market-driven media industries, not 'Newspeak', but is the effect far different? Where there can be no debate, there can be no politics. Thus the epigraph from Orwell at the start of this chapter, which speaks to me of nothing so much as the inability of our major parties to see beyond specific grievances, since they are equally unable to see beyond Fukuyama's liberal internationalism. But who is it, in our context, that staffs the 'Ministry of Truth'?

The last part of this story concerns the specialists in ideas.[71] Belief in applied knowledge has stimulated an increasing resort to specialists who speak not from their knowledge of the community or of politics, but from their expertise. Professionals advocating particular programs have regularly cropped up on the fringes of government.[72] Of late, however, such people have been drawn into the centre, with perceptible effects on the public culture. In part, 'experts' have been drawn in by the pressure on politicians to appear attuned to the complex intellectual demands of the modern world. Informal practices by leaders of creating 'private office' families for personal support have everywhere become institutionalised.[73] This was only one face of the resort to specialist advice. The public service more broadly was transformed in the 1980s to promote managerial and economic efficiency and in ways that accentuated the particular intellectual agenda we've explored.[74] Suddenly people with narrow specialisms had considerable sway, not just at the ministers' sides, but in the public service generally. The specialisms most frequently favoured were management and economics.

A process that commenced with informal networks has ended with the dominance of institutionalised, in-house, technical specialists. The needs for informed decision making and for specialist skills in a modern polity are clear. But when every political problem is seen as demanding a technical solution the shortcomings become evident. Instead of listening to the community and attempting to respond to its needs, political leaders swing to telling the community what it should have or do. The swing, increasingly away from persuasion— Menzies' call to the 'forgotten people', Whitlam's call to the 'men and women of Australia'—to prescription—Keating perhaps most famously on the 'recession we had to have'—in modern political rhetoric has been remarkable.

It's not that politicians have been at the mercy of their advisers. Rather, it has been a symbiotic process, one of collusion, where politicians who are too caught up in the exigencies of combat politics to devise solutions have been provided with ready-made answers by the dominant intellectual movement of the day. That this is a moment when everything is seen to hinge on a specialist form of economic knowledge, and one apparently devoid of any sense of history or of the collective interest, reveals the potential shortcoming of the intellectuals. They can be too specialised, too much the creatures of their context and their political masters, incapable of taking the long view.

The capacity for broad social criticism was also inhibited by features of contemporary intellectual life quite other than its proclivity towards a specialist focus combined with a general ignorance. Not just in the Liberal Party, but also on the right generally, the conservative idea of an organic community was comprehensively routed by economic individualism. While there has been some return of community-minded conservatism, evident, for instance, in the criticisms of economic rationalism, and of Hewson and his ilk, by the *Quadrant* intellectuals, this has typically been backward looking and sentimental, appealing to the characteristics of a world that cannot be regained.[75]

Yet the left intelligentsia was equally incapable of offering an alternative. For too many, the 'liberating' agendas of post modernism—a project that speaks out for difference and diversity against the oppressively unifying constraints of modernity—precluded any effective politics. Left intellectuals, prone to seeing every form of unifying statement as oppressive and every form of authority (even social authority) as hostile, started by advocating post modernism and a subversive libertarianism and ended by celebrating the market as the best means of giving people what they wanted. Post modernism, like free market economics, has difficulty in imagining / civil society. Post modernism assumes that 'fragmentation' and the abandonment of universals, along with the assertion of plurality and diversity of choice, are the means of subverting dominant hierarchies of values. But does this adequately understand the universalisation of economic structures in modern societies? Against the popularity of post modernism, Anthony Giddens reminds us that:

> some have . . . presumed that . . . fragmentation marks the
> emergence of a novel phase of social development . . . a
> post-modern era. Yet the unifying features of modern
> institutions are just as central to modernity . . . processes that
> established a single 'world' where none existed previously.[76]

Financial markets are what now bind the 'single world' together. The problem is that that 'single world' is not the world of a small country like Australia, hostage to the world economy.

In the single world of the capitalist market, where transnational corporations are uniquely placed to control the capital-intensive technologies of mass communication, and international financial markets can discipline unruly states, how are particular, regional, and local communities to take control? Not through the questions that concern the post modern left. Terry Eagleton argues that the 'playful irony' of post modernism 'is more likely to play into the hands of the ruling powers than to discomfort them'. We may be cynical, knowing, ironic, but we cannot act:

if political practice takes place only within a context of interpretation, and if that context is notoriously ambiguous and unstable, then action itself is likely to be problematic and unpredictable.[77]

Meanwhile, the world market will continue its universalising practices unchecked, decisions will be driven largely by commercial imperatives (limiting, rather than opening up, choices), and the chances of particular communities taking control of their economies, or of the modern technologies that mediate their popular cultures, will be lost.

In an earlier era, Australians believed that there were choices, and that when policies failed to deliver, insistence on government action could achieve change. Since then, we seem to have lost the plot, and the emphasis has shifted from political action to elite prescription. But is that a measure of how wrong those earlier activists were, or a measure of how far we have fallen victim to a 'single world' which seems to offer us everything—everything but community, or the means to articulate our own political visions?

CHAPTER 6

Constructive
alternatives

The politics I've described depends on choices. But what choices do we have? It's all very well to show that the decisions taken in the recent past have not delivered what was promised, but what else could we do? How can we answer Hawke's assertion, that 'if the world doesn't trust you it can destroy you'? Well, first we must be persuaded that there *are* economic alternatives. And, second, we must find grounds to believe that we can take charge of our own affairs, that we are *not* simply subject to the caprice of 'the international market'.

Let me take a limited example, again from the British context. The development strategy that proved disastrous in Docklands (see chapters 1 and 4), was also considered for other parts of London. The ways in which it was resisted in Spitalfields provide an illuminating comparison. It was said that Spitalfields was in decline, that being so close to the city it could be more productively employed, that the product of the local community (Bengali garment makers in the main) was marginal and couldn't compete in the new Europe. But the local community refused to be pushed aside, insisted on the viability of its own economic product and created a business enhancing community association to foster it. With the assistance of sympathetic lawyers and planners, it utilised planning regulations to force state agencies to recognise its claims and to negotiate with it. This was not a form of 'natural socialism'—most of the members of the community association were fiercely independent small businesses, but they recognised their common interests. The ambitions of the developers were thus delayed until the Docklands bubble burst. By then local activism had regenerated the Spitalfields community, and its economy. But, it will be said, a neighbourhood is not the same as a country (even if the country, too, is small, with a marginal economic output, unable to 'compete'). The detail, however, is not important: the lesson is that a way forward might be found if economic productivity is linked with a people's vision of common interest and a willingness to mobilise to force the agencies of the state to respond. That said, we can expect the assertion of common interests and the demand for state action to meet vigorous opposition from the guardians of contemporary orthodoxies.

The challenge of globalising capitalism

While writing this book I published a fragment of my argument in a brief newspaper article.[1] This evoked an immediate response from Wolfgang Kasper, an economist who had been early in the field in arguing for the necessity of dismantling protection and internationalising the economy.[2] My attempts to foster debate about political (rather than economic) ideas, he said, 'betray(ed) a considerable nostalgia for a world in which political action was decisive and took priority over economic life'.[3] His argument, one we have met in earlier chapters (see, especially, chapter 3), was that the world has changed fundamentally, that the great unifying ideas belonged to an era when 'the nation state was reasonably closed and social engineers could try to implement cohesive political visions'. In the 'open' world of the present 'owners of high technical and organisational skills, of capital and of technical knowhow, have become highly mobile amongst nations'. Confronted with political demands, or with 'footing the bill for income redistribution; being regulated away from their aspirations', these people 'will simply take the economic option of walking away and placing their assets elsewhere'. Political actions, even political ideas, are thus undermined:

> Political commentators and leaders who try to recreate the past when political ideas had primacy are not likely to win the day, even if they offer us the comfort of a return to the familiar. Political leaders who grasp the full implications of the fundamental technical and economic shifts of the past decade and who develop a political culture that attracts mobile productive resources are likely to command the future.

My central objective is, as Kasper rightly discerns, to rethink the conditions in which political action *can* be decisive and will take priority over economic life. Why? Because the market left unconstrained does not deliver even what it promises; the market unmediated by politics creates wealth at the cost of community and society, as chapter 4 shows. This revival of politics will not involve simply adopting ideas from the past, but rather identifying the processes through which political thinking itself can be resuscitated. Kasper raises exactly the questions that must be countered if such processes are to be retrieved: are political projects luxuries only thinkable within a closed state? Is political 'vision' always related to social engineering? Is the 'discipline' exercised by those who control capital, technology, knowledge and administrative skills as untramelled (by politics or community) as Kasper believes? This boils down to a foundational question: can a particular geo-political community (such as Australia) strike its own terms in dealing with the world economy?

The history we have reviewed suggests two lessons: that state command economies fail, and that 'free market' economies will frustrate the expectations we have developed about them. There must be mediation of the 'free' market in the interests of the community, and that mediation will be by agencies of the state acting for the community. That is to say, there should be political direction in economic life, and there should be a mixed economy. But, the critics will say, that is precisely where we were in the 1950s and 1960s, this *is* nothing more than a recapitulation of strategies that have failed. Our first task then is to ask: can there be a newly relevant defence of the mixed economy? And the crucial test of its relevance will be: can it operate within the global economy?

The persistence of the mixed economy

Despite the claims of economic liberalisation and internationalisation, governments have not left, and cannot leave, the scene. The size of commercial enterprise in the modern world means governments must be involved. Here is an example. At a lunch I attended with business people in London in 1992, conversation turned to ways of private enterprise funding of a new airport in Hong Kong. Finally, the chairman of a major airline with extensive coverage of Asian routes (the only relevant industry figure present) intervened: 'No private interest, no consortium of private interests, is likely to make an investment on the huge scale needed for that airport. If they want us to fly there, if they want the tourists and their world city status to continue, the government will have to build the airport.' Or take another instance: even though it has been a market failure, the Docklands development in London (see chapter 1) was initiated by the government creating 'enterprise zones', and huge amounts of public money subsidised the experiment.[4] Similar, if less spectacular, patterns characterise the development of Melbourne's Docklands and Sydney's Darling Harbour. Such accommodations between government and business are a central part of Australian economic history, as Butlin and others remind us,[5] and they are now integral to modern commerce worldwide. Further, markets are not, and have never been, autonomous—they require the frameworks provided by the state to exist. Governments maintain a legal order, control the spheres in which markets operate, define the nature of business practice, regulate and stabilise the labour market, determine access to natural resources, influence money supply and ensure the social stability without which commerce cannot proceed. Even global markets depend on these base conditions: while big players can move across the world to take advantage of the most favourable conjunctions of governance for their purposes, they cannot function if those conditions created by the actions of states do not exist at all. States secure the conditions under which markets can operate. This may seem to be labouring the obvious, but so dominant has been the rhetoric of the market that we are encouraged to believe that we must choose between the state or the market, rather than imagining interdependence between them.

New defences of the mixed economy

There are constructive alternatives to contemporary economic orthodoxy. They eschew the false choice between the state and the market and concentrate instead on the nature of their interdependence.

Examples of active coalitions of state and commercial interests in contemporary economies are easy to discover— examples, that is, which do not belong to the superseded 'protectionist' age to which economic rationalists would like to relegate alternative views. The late Tom Fitzgerald instanced Japan's achievement of economic superpower status. That achievement depended upon a directed economy; clearly articulated industrial policy; close relations between state bureaucracies and industrial sectors through the Ministry of International Trade and Industry (MITI); close cooperation between management and banks; consultative policy councils; selective protection; control of investment; financial stimulus (with a terminal date) to selected industries, along with assistance in contraction and consolidation of declining industries, thus facilitating economic change; strategic overseas investment, facilitating the diversification of sources of supply; and so on.[6] Despite emerging economic problems—driven as much by bilateral trading difficulties with the US as by anything internal—Japan remains a managed economy, determined to avoid the scale of market failures and social problems (especially unemployment) that dog Western economies.[7] The newly industrialising countries (NICs) of Asia have learned from Japan, and sustain interventionist forms of managed capitalism. While liberal triumphalists like Fukuyama persist in regarding the NICs as transitional, on the road to 'free markets', what the Japanese example shows is that this can be a long-term pattern, designed to be responsive to, rather than an impediment in, the global economy—a point to which I will return. Within a polity in which we are constantly told to look to Asia (see chapter 2), it is surprising that the Asian growth economies have not stimulated more open debate on ways of managing capitalism for social and economic ends.

There is also the European corporatist model of negotiation between the state, producer groups and labour within social markets. Geoff Dow, in reassessing the Australian case in comparison with European economies, argues:

> Good economic performance, especially over the past seventeen years, has depended on institutional arrangements that have been labelled 'corporatist'. The literature . . . that has criticised corporatism for its violation of liberal or parliamentary niceties therefore seems to have missed the point. Such arrangements have been effective at maintaining the security and living standards of the subject populations; liberal institutions have not . . . what they achieve in a general sense is an extension of the range of decisions subject to political determination. When the organisations of capital or of labour are forced to participate publicly in decision-making that previously took place privately, *the realm of politics expands*.[8] [emphasis added]

Dow argues for more clear-cut political control of investment decisions, a permanent determination of income distribution and a long-term 'decommodified' labour market policy.[9] To achieve such political intervention in the market will require an effective state. Australia (in comparison with economically successful European polities) has been dragged back by the systematic underdevelopment of public institutions throughout the twentieth century.[10] This has left us with 'a depleted ability to deal with the social and economic consequences of economic restructuring when it needs to occur'.[11] This is not an argument for a closed system, but rather for a system that can respond and restructure where necessary, yet in terms where political considerations as well as market needs can take effect.

In a critical response to Dow, Brian Dollery insists on the pervasiveness of government or non market failure, and—predictably (see Kasper, Kelly, Fukuyama *et al.* above)—that internationalisation makes the option of (to use Dow's words) 'institutional determination of economic development' within a state impossible.[12] To make the first point is to ignore Dow's evidence of circumstances where states *have not* failed, but have successfully directed their own economic development. Tom Fitzgerald's impassioned argument, John Langmore and John Quiggin's comparative analysis of national employment strategies[13] and a body of other persuasive contemporary work,[14] support Dow's contention. Liberal critics conflate the collapse of the command economies with arguments against state action *per se*, as a strategy for avoiding debate about successful state participation in capitalist economies. If some countries have been better able to resist the forces of the international economy, or at least to turn them into opportunities rather than constraints, why is this? Dow shows that economic decisions are inevitably political in their effects, and it is therefore legitimate to demand that they be openly politicised. Negotiation between the state, labour and capital establishes the process where the political can emerge. For our purposes, it might be said to be the precondition for the revival of political imagination. The question then is, in what circumstances, in what kinds of capitalist economy, has state intervention succeeded both in positively influencing economic development, and in securing political ends?

There is no one model. Dow's preferred model is Sweden, with favourable comparisons as well with Norway, Austria, Luxembourg, Finland, Switzerland and Japan. He acknowledges, too, 'failure among some of the countries to have chosen a "big government" route to development', such as Belgium, Italy, the Netherlands, Denmark and France.[15] The point is to distinguish successful from unsuccessful models. The successful models had these characteristics: an institutionalised commitment to full employment; restructuring as part of an ongoing process in which a state capacity to resist capricious adjustments had already been established; and a capacity to create new industries or new activities from which new national capacities and competences can be developed.[16] Tom Fitzgerald, as we saw, draws lessons from the industrialisation of Japan and the NICs. William Keegan, in a book that extends elements of both Dow's and Fitzgerald's arguments, offers a sustained comparison of Japan's 'industrial capitalism', the German 'social market economy' and our poorly performing Anglo–Saxon 'dealer capitalism'.[17] Keegan and Dow produce the economic analysis to show that economies aspiring towards untramelled market theory and unlimited managerial prerogative do not necessarily perform better, and the policy analysis to show that a range of social institutions going well beyond the minimalist state contribute to economic success. While utterly clear on the failure of communism, Keegan argues forcefully that 'the survival of the market economies may, paradoxically, have to be carefully planned'.[18] As for surviving in the modern world, Keegan shows that the short termism of 'dealer capitalism' cannot generate and support complex, technology-driven quality products and processes.

John Langmore and John Quiggin have demonstrated just what such planning might mean in the Australian case. The serious problem of unemployment, they show, cannot be dealt with by palliative measures within a framework where economic policy is still governed by liberal internationalism. Instead, it has to be integral to a national economic program. The program will depend upon economic growth along with active state intervention, and on increased public expenditure along with regaining control of the financial sector:

> The key element is a return to active government intervention, through macroeconomic policy, increased provision of community services and increased investment in social and physical infrastructure. A macroeconomic strategy oriented towards growth would be based on the flexible use of fiscal stimulus, in response to the needs of the economy. This would entail acceptance of the need for large deficits in recession periods, with the use of tax policy to generate surpluses in periods of full employment. Active fiscal policy must be combined with a reassertion of control over the financial system, to make it the servant, rather than the master of the real economy . . . These proposals . . . would involve a major

stimulus to the private sector, both directly through increased demand and indirectly through improvements in physical and human services. The proposed net increases in government expenditure would be less than three per cent of GDP and would still leave Australia as one of the lowest taxing, lowest-spending countries in the OECD, with a similarly low level of public debt.[19]

Against the strident objections of economic rationalism, this wise book goes into sober detail about how such a program might be achieved. Its advantage is that it is deeply rooted in the details of the Australian case, showing that we do not have to be (*pace* Dow and Keegan) entirely reliant on extraneous models, helpful as these are. Its gift is to reveal that alternative strategies are not only thinkable, but do-able. But its important message is that this will involve political will. The question remains, how do we revive political will?

A mixed economy in the global market

Given that most of these arguments concern action within nation states, do they provide an answer to the objection that economic internationalisation erodes the ability of states to manage their economies? We should not forget that the desire of financial agencies to operate within particular national markets still gives the nation some leverage. Access should be balanced by obligations, and Langmore and Quiggin show how this can be used to reintroduce 'an appropriate system of prudential regulation'.[20] A view is emerging that the centrality of international competition may be overstated, that the rhetoric of competitiveness has become 'a dangerous obsession', and that the idea that a country's economic features are largely determined by its success on world markets is wrong.[21] 'Even though world trade is larger than ever before, national living standards are overwhelmingly determined by domestic factors.' In part, the world is not as interdependent as has been argued (the US, for instance, is still almost 90 per cent an economy that produces goods and services for its own use); in part, countries simply aren't in head to head competition: '. . . the major industrial economies, while they sell products that compete with each other, are also each other's main export markets and each other's main suppliers of useful imports'. International trade is not a zero-sum game: Japanese growth, for instance, is not at the expense of the US quality of life.[22] Liberal internationalism's competitive rhetoric drastically oversimplifies.

Governments may enter into careful market planning to capitalise upon opportunities in the international market—which was the crux of Fitzgerald's case about Japan. Hugh Emy has elaborated upon this argument.[23] He contends that trading conditions have diverged from the assumptions underpinning neo-classical economics (the norm is not general equilibrium but oligopolistic competition), and that modern high-tech manufacturing depends less on comparative advantage (availability of labour, capital or raw materials) and more on infrastructure (R & D, creativity and knowledge). Infrastructure, research, knowledge production—these are the realms of government, so there is 'more scope . . . for governments to intervene to improve the resource base or provide the enabling conditions likely to attract and/or advantage globally competitive industries within its [sic] own territory'.[24] Drawing on strategic trade theory and that of competitive advantage, Emy sketches conditions for productive government intervention—where production or export subsidies, tax concessions, tariff or non-tariff barriers might encourage firms to produce in a strategic area they would otherwise assess as too uncertain to enter; or where intervention might improve a domestic firm's share of the local market in order to provide it with the capacity to export at lower prices; or where governments can create cultural and institutional conditions to stimulate companies to pursue competitive advantage, 'pushing companies to take new initiatives or to raise their performance'.[25]

Governments can contribute with strategic vision, infrastructural assistance, promotion of sustained investment, and enforcement of product, safety and environment standards, while recognising that intervention, too, entails risks. Governments must not shield firms, but improve their competitiveness; they must not preclude rivalry; they must not only endure but also facilitate structural change.

> One cannot go with the flow because no one knows quite where the flow is going. Some degree of foresight, strategic planning or collective response is required. It is time to be improving both the quality of government and the institutional capacity of the state, especially in regard to economic development and industrial policy, rather than dismantling it holus-bolus in the name of small government . . .
>
> Outside Australia it is less a question of minimising the state and the possibilities of state intervention and more a matter of asking what sorts of selective intervention are now required to build or sustain a competitive market economy, one which will also prove durable in the face of rising global pressures . . . Overall . . . in nearly all leading industrial nations, some kind of deliberate industry policy, involving . . . national strategies built around close cooperation between business and government to gain world market share in selected industries, is seen as a necessary and inevitable response to the competitive pressures released by globalisation.[26]

To return to Keegan's point, the survival of markets may depend on such planning.

Emy opts for the German 'social market model' as that best suited to inspire the kind of rethinking needed in Australia.[27] The general point, however, is that 'countries with distinctly communitarian value systems, especially Japan, Germany and other Asian and European societies, have adapted more successfully to the heightened pace of international competition . . .'[28] because there the different parts of society will work collectively, flexibly in devising new institutions. The Anglo–Liberal, individualistic cultures, in contrast, persist with attitudes 'which undermine social cooperation and prevent the development of concerted adaptive strategies'[29]. Reviewing these arguments gives ground for saying, 'surely "best practice" examples of a sophisticated mixing of state action and market forces in both economically effective and socially supportive ways is the lesson of contemporary comparative political economy'.[30]

What about the final plaint, that the very thought of 'mixing state action and market forces' in the Anglo–Liberal cultures will induce capital flight, and the emigration of high-earning holders of technical, fiscal and knowledge skills? The untramelled exercise of such 'freedoms' might devastate national economies. Yet there are logical constraints which such an argument overlooks. Investment follows resources—not just primary resources, but resources like a sophisticated infrastructure; a reliable, educated, skilled workforce; a properly regulated market; a predictable legal system. This gives the community in possession of such resources some leverage (the markets won't 'destroy' you if there is still something to be gained from you). Investment, if it is to be secure, is driven not only by profit but also by stability. Politically stable democracies are a better long-term bet for capital accumulation than countries where civil disorder threatens the legal structure of markets. Rapid and unpredictable disinvestment, to the extent that it threatens social conditions, and induces chaos within certain states, might over time reduce the pool of stable investment opportunities, inexorably reducing the options of 'walking away'. As for those flighty transnational knowledge elites, only if they came from Canberra could they imagine that their quality of life would improve in the 'free market' metropolises. There is a significant literature on the flight of professionals from New York, Los Angeles, London, Paris and so on, not because they have been taxed, or 'regulated away from their aspirations', but because of issues of safety, ghettoisation and deteriorating infrastructure in the 'market' city. The best of these studies, such as Mike Davis's of Los Angeles,[31] show that these professionals can buy safety (at the cost of living in segregated ghettoes); that the public domain can be secured (by being 'privatised', and at the cost of high levels of surveillance); that the streets can be made 'safe' (by para-military levels of policing)—and that every such strategy reduces freedoms. For many, the high salaries flowing from their transferable skills are no compensation for the loss of such freedoms. Where, then, are they to 'walk' to?

Answers to the economists

In essence, each of the questions Kasper's objections gave rise
to, can be productively answered in ways that point to constructive alternatives. We do not need to look back to a golden
age of protection to defend the mixed economy—contemporary examples of economic success fostered by an active state
abound. Planning is not tied either to closed systems or to
social engineering: it can be cooperative, adaptive and predi-
cated on continual change. At its best, it is attuned to gaining
strategic advantage in the international market rather than
erecting barriers against it. A *concerted* adaptive strategy,
demands that the state is, and must be, an economic player
in its own right. The economic success of such strategies, as
demonstrated by the more communitarian economies, is itself
the warranty for state intervention. But if the state is to be
such a player, it must retain planning capacities, it must aim
not for deregulation, but for better regulation[32]—and it is these
capacities that Australian governments have seemed intent on
giving away.

These alternatives to free market orthodoxies, and
defences of a newly relevant mixed economy, are necessary
conditions for the revival of politics. Only when alternatives
are aired and when the 'one big idea' is challenged and we
recognise that social life is about debate rather than prescription, can political imagination re-emerge. Knowing the
answers to the economic rationalists gives us necessary
ammunition in asserting the importance of debate, but it is
not sufficient in itself. If it was, the economic would be giving
way before the political much faster than appears to be the
case. Why isn't this happening? Partly, it is because alternative
voices can gain little space in the mass media, and are thus
denied the standpoint from which they might influence the
public culture.[33] But, more importantly, it is the outcome of
the process Fukuyama describes: the dominance of liberal
economics has impeded confidence in any other intellectual
tools, the conflation of all aspects of social life with the market
has swept away all vantage points outside the market. If
politics is about mediation between the state and the market

in the interests of community, if it is about negotiating the nature of the interdependence between the state and the market, then it depends on a realm beyond either of them. It depends on rethinking community and the nature of those ties between people constituted neither by government nor by economic exchange.

CHAPTER 7

Reviving political
imagination

Where do we go from here? I have argued that the commitment to a monistic worldview in economic rationalism has eviscerated politics. Competing ideas have been marginalised in public debate. Yet the last chapter shows that some thinkers have not lost sight of alternatives, and have continued to argue for an interaction between politics and economics (rather than accepting that political action is entirely dictated by economic necessities). If they have not been heard, it is not because this debate has no substance, but because we've lost sight of the conditions for debate.

What do I mean by the conditions for debate? Consider this: if I am thinking of how to put something right, how to argue for something better, in an everyday social context, what are likely to be the pertinent considerations? First, the issue must mean something to me. Second, I will need some idea, some picture, of how things might be improved. Third, I must believe that at least some of those with whom I am involved share common interests in the issue. Fourth, I am unlikely to speak at all if there is no chance of being heard—if I am not given a voice. Fifth, I may not take the trouble if, despite some chance of winning the argument, there are no processes through which better ideas can be put into effect. The substance of the debate, then, will be an idea, but the conditions for the debate will be a series of judgments about its meaning for me, an audience with shared interests (and which will listen), and processes through which changes can be made.

It's easy enough for most of us, I'd suggest, to recall cases in our own contexts—school, association, workplace, community group, or the like—where such considerations have played a part in our decision to pursue (or to drop) an issue. But how do we translate these ways of thinking into the politics of the public domain? Well, it is clear that at one level we've already done so: it is exactly the sense that politics carries no personal meanings, that there are no fresh ideas, that little that we can do will make a difference and that if we speak we will not be heard, that fosters the disillusion Mackay and others report (see the introduction).

My purpose in this chapter, however, is to suggest that we can restore the conditions of political debate by recovering a place to stand in the public domain. How? In the workplace, in pursuing an issue, I might take my stand as a colleague, appeal to your common interest in our shared enterprise, speak of loyalty to the firm (or at least of our material interest in seeing the firm prosper). In the public domain, however, the process is both more abstract and more difficult: I can take my stand as a citizen, insist on the society's interests being served, and appeal to national loyalties—but each of these terms is thrown into question by the processes considered in this book. Is citizenship a matter of consumer rights? Can a society be recognised amongst the many voices claiming a right to speak? Has the nation succumbed to economic globalisation? Despite these difficulties, however, I will argue here that we need to recapture ways of thinking about citizen, society and nation to restore the conditions for political debate. We must re-establish a place to stand—a ground for social relations that goes beyond either state or market—before ideas will flow, and debate be restored. The meanings we attach to 'citizen', 'community' (or 'society') will be the components of that ground. And political imagination will be revived not by one or two grand ideas, but by thus recovering the processes that underwrite politics.

Rethinking citizenship

It would be easy to see the recent revival of discussion about citizenship in Australia as being dependent on initiatives of the former Labor government (such as its establishment of a Civics Expert Group) and therefore as no longer relevant. It would also be profoundly mistaken. Increased preoccupation with citizenship has been a phenomenon in all Western (and in newly democratising) polities, not just in Australia. From Eastern Europe to the former Thatcherite think-tanks of England (see below), there has been rethinking of citizenship and civil society as people seek a new ground for politics and a new language of cohesion. There are general pressures behind this—the breakdown of old ties of community, the impact of political disillusionment, the increased circulation of peoples—and they are pressures any government must manage. Whatever John Howard's reluctance to adopt something embraced by Paul Keating, the worldwide renaissance of citizenship debates means that they will remain in the public eye in the long term. Soon after their election in 1996, Coalition ministers showed signs of recognising this (renewing discussion on the nature of the citizenship oath, for instance).

It is no accident that our political and cultural elites, concerned about the tenor of politics, have resorted to the consideration of civics and citizenship as a way of raising our game. Citizenship is the most basic way of talking about the links between an individual and the community—and our leaders seek to encourage active engagement of individuals in the community to counter disillusion. Of course, it has long been a standard move in political rhetoric to suggest that 'good citizens' will, as a matter of duty, act in the terms suggested by one's argument. We might well regard the resort to 'citizenship' with cynicism. It is worth suspending disbelief, however, while we re-examine how the discussion of citizenship is always a discussion of (and reminds us of the potentials of) the most basic bargain in politics.

Citizenship is a way of talking about entitlements: the things which you are guaranteed by nationality, by belonging.

But it is also a way of talking about responsibility: the things which you are obliged to do to preserve the public good. In Australia, both aspects are neatly captured in the franchise: a citizen is not only entitled to vote (to pursue or express political wishes), but also legally obliged to vote (mass democracy is deemed a public good). Citizenship may mean different things in different nations: there is no neat formula about the precise mix of entitlements and responsibilities.

There is a hierarchy of possible citizen rights. We have become accustomed to thinking of three categories of rights— civil rights (rights related to individual freedom, such as freedom of speech and religion, freedom of contract, the right to own property, the entitlement to just treatment); political rights (the right to form and to join associations, the right to stand for and be an elector to democratic legislatures); and social rights (the right to security, ensured through welfare provisions).[1] Every society will differ in the degree to which these rights are recognised and the ways in which they are blended. Not all members of a society necessarily enjoy the same access to such rights: men and women, whites and blacks did not receive citizenship rights at the same time within Australia, for instance.[2] But the assumption is that in the long run, citizenship is about equality: over time civil rights engender political and social rights, and these spread to encompass more and more people.

Historically, we can see that there has been differential accessibility to citizen entitlements (on class, gender and ethnic grounds).[3] But it is worth saying that if citizenship has been gendered, class-based and ethnically biased, it does not have to continue to be so. The distinctions between different sorts of rights provide ways of thinking about different aspects of citizenship, the way they might be mixed and sustained, and their historical specifics in particular contexts.

Citizenship is provisional. It is legally defined and institutionalised, but it should be regarded as always under negotiation. It encapsulates the bargain of the individual with the nation: what must I do for the collective, what am I entitled to demand? Thus, it is the fundamental bargain in politics: the point where we draw the line. Conventions and legality can defend it only up to a point, beyond that must be political activism. We might, for example, regard freedom of movement in the public domain as having the status of a civil right. But in a context where cities are increasingly allowing the privatisation of once public spaces (the environs of shopping centres, for instance), people can find themselves unwittingly subject to surveillance, unwillingly subject to direction and unexpectedly subject to ejection.[4] Protest and dissent, in such a case, can itself be deemed illegal, a trespass contrary to the laws of property. If the legal status of such a civil right is to be extended, it will only be through politics. We can be sure, though, that other citizens, faced with such a movement, will argue the pre-eminence of property rights over those of freedom of movement. The overriding point is that what citizen rights are to be, will depend upon political settlements.

The tenor of politics will depend heavily upon the nature of the balance between individual commitment to the public good (citizen obligations) and individual rights (citizen entitlements). One tradition has it that the test of a good citizen is the ability to put aside private interests in deciding where the public good lies.[5] But the Fukuyama style of liberalism, by putting individual interests first, subordinates politics to private gain: in Anne Phillips words, '[t]he idea that politics is about the pursuit of public happiness or the taste of public freedom has been tossed aside as an archaic ideal'.[6]

In Australia, this has involved the diminution of those social rights contained in what Kelly derides as the Australian settlement. Why has there not been a stronger defence? In part because of disillusion with the efficacy of politics, in a context where we were told we had no options. Citizen rights were no more than consumer rights in a privatised social sphere. But in part, too, because citizenship has not been a leading concern in our political culture. An Anglophone settler society, we are described in our constitution as subjects within a monarchy, rather than as sovereign people capable of the self-determination citizenship entails. As a settler society, confronted with the need to build new institutions, it may be that we have been more preoccupied with the sorts of behaviours these institutions need to survive than with how they should serve individuals. On this argument, perhaps the state has defined who we are, and there has not been a self-constituted citizenry.[7] In other words, those concerned with the processes which will make national government work come up with institutional procedures and definitions which govern the ways in which we 'imagine' ourselves a people. This bureaucratic dominance might explain why our strongest resort to citizenship rhetoric is provoked by objections to being treated as 'second-class citizens'.[8] That aside, citizenship has been seen only in the weak sense (as something akin to patriotism), or in the legal sense (the avowals required of those immigrants seeking naturalisation). Active citizenship, conceived as a political settlement guaranteeing certain rights, and spelling out the bargain between citizen and nation, has been rare in Australia. So we must build it.

This sense of active citizenship is fundamental to a proper national politics. A clear program of citizen rights serves as a check on both the state and the market. It is an expression of the sort of society we want. The debate about civil rights, and the preservation of individual freedoms, sets the limits on state activity. The debate about citizen obligations defines what we should individually be prepared to sacrifice for the public good (determining levels of regulation, taxation and so on). The debate about social rights sets the limits of markets, for if there is acceptance of universal entitlement to, say, a certain level of health care, state agencies will have to act if there is market failure (the market, for instance, has not served Aboriginal health needs—since they cannot afford to 'buy' what they need). To make these simple points is to presume nothing about the links between obligation and entitlement, about the balance between civil, political and social rights— these will always be matters for negotiation, for political settlement. The nature of the settlement will determine what it means to be Australian.

This sort of citizenship is not derived from blood or land, class or gender. It is a political identity. Being political, it is not static. It will, for many, continue to be acquired by birth— but it should be ensured by active identification with the processes of political settlement particular to the community. That entails civic education: citizen competences are formed through understanding the institutions, processes and choices that brought us to the present, and how such processes may be deployed in pursuit of different futures. It is not an exclusive identity: people of other origins can opt in to our political settlement by assuming the obligations this entails. And it is not an identity that assumes homogeneity: it can contain diversity, difference, social pluralism, because it contends only that we should have common rights and entitlements, and that (for all our many differences) we are, at the political level, 'a community of fate',[9] sharing a common destiny. What that destiny is to be is not ordained, it is instead to be achieved through politics.

Rethinking civil society

So much for one element in the political bargain. A citizen, however, is not a free floating entity, and everything I say above presupposes that citizenship can only be understood *as* a social factor, a settlement achieved within a particular society. In this age of fragmentation, we should not take this other part of the equation for granted.

It is useful to speak of the sphere of social relations outside both state and market as civil society.[10] Here is where we live most of our lives, not in politics or citizenly rituals, but in the social networks and associations of the 'real world'. In our pubs and clubs and committees and associations and workplace unions and churches and so on, we find the networks that give life meaning, the places where our input and decisions can be seen to matter. Here, ideally, we learn the importance of connecting with others, and of responsibility. Here is where the meaning of citizenship should be instilled.

Until recently such ideas were eclipsed by the growth of the state on one hand, and by the triumphalism of free enterprise on the other. They have lately been pushed to the fore again. Political thinkers from Eastern Europe have argued that civil society—a life apart from the state—was destroyed by communist regimes and must now be rebuilt again. Curiously, from another vantage, some of the former advocates of free market ideas now concede that they may have gone too far in emphasising the economy at the expense of community, and suggest that civil society must be 'reinvented'.[11] They suggest, however, that civil society's resilience was eroded by the welfare state, which undercut the voluntarism on which healthy associations thrive, and they see economic exchange as unproblematically a part of civil society, which exists against the state. If our aim is social solidarity, though, it makes sense to think of civil society as in some degree against both state and market, for, as we have seen, economic dislocation is as destructive of social solidarity as state intrusion.[12]

We need the idea of civil society to remind us that we are social beings before we are either political or economic beings. We need it, too, to remind us that: 'the people have an identity, they have purposes, even . . . a will, outside of any political structure'.[13] But do we inherit civil society, or do we build it? One view is that the patterns of civil society emerge 'naturally' from the congeries of voluntary associations at a society's 'grassroots'. What if, as I suggest above, people come together and, through a conscious process of determining administrative principles in building political institutions, come to generate their own paradigm of the civil society?[14] It may be a mistake to assume that 'a people', whose will is expressed through voluntary associations, exists prior to political or economic structures. We do, each of us, have a life outside politics and economics, but it may be the frustrations of politics and economics that bring 'the people' to life, by reminding us of our interdependence, of the respects in which we either suffer, or prosper, together.

Think, for example, of Australian Federation. Did an Australian 'people' exist before Federation? The federal conventions, the drawing up of the constitution, the negotiation and building up of popular support, were all public acts, a self-evident case of institution building. The historical record is clear: we know how it was done, and who were the players. This makes it hard to argue that the constitution that emerged was an expression of the will of 'the people'. Some, indeed, have seen it as a sell-out to the British empire,[15] others as a manifestation of a continuing bourgeois hegemony (and the dominance of lawyers).[16] Certainly there were winners and losers, but Charles Blackton showed thirty years ago that the winners were not knee-jerk empire loyalists, but nativist moderates intent on such national sovereignty as could be achieved within the economic relations of empire.[17]

If you want a contemporary parallel, think of the ways Paul Keating recently tried to balance nationalist rhetoric with the 'necessity' of Australian economic integration with Asia. It is more sensible, as Helen Irving argues, to recognise that the federalists could not have been radical nationalists 'since there was simply not the public will to support a radical or republican constitution'. Instead the federalists provided the means by which the Australian nation could 'imagine itself both as part of the community of the Empire, and at the same time as sovereign'.[18] The Federation debates were of course about politics and economy, but they were also at a more muted level debates about civil society—the sort of society Australia should become, the place of economic exchange, the appropriate limits of state action. This was to set the stage on which the citizen could act. And, as Irving shows, the federal imaginary became the popular imaginary: a people and a civil society both found definition in the process.

The ways of thinking appropriate to the 1890s may not serve well in the 1990s. But let us not reinvent those times in our own image. Let us learn from them, instead, that civil society can be defined in the process of institution building, and does not emanate from some mysteriously removed 'people's' domain. We should recognise, too, that civil society can be found not only by looking back (to some illusion of a pre-political 'people') but also by looking forward (to the sort of society we want).

History and tradition are important ways of talking about community, but the resort to tradition is no defence against capitalism (indeed, Marx, in a brilliant passage from the *Communist Manifesto*, shows tradition to be one of the first things to be swept away).[19] The defence of civil society, therefore, should be based not on appeals to family, tradition, the

'Australian character' and so on, but on arguments synthesising what is valuable in our past with what is our best hope for the future. That is exactly what Irving shows to be going on in the Federation debates of the 1890s.

A persuasive representation of civil society, then, will rest not on tradition or heritage, but on arguments invoking principles.[20] These will be principles of community. And it is here that we may strike a snag. Some would argue that the possibility of there now being a community to which people are committed is the faintest hope of all:

> Societies today have a rich and not always harmonious variety of people with different ethnic backgrounds, religious identifications, moral outlooks, political orientations and class positions. There is not much reality to the melting pot or vertical mosaic metaphors of the United States and Canada, respectively. There is no chance at all that in such societies there could ever be anything like a functioning conception of a common good . . . There is simply no chance of there being a general consensus of the various people that inhabit these societies. Pluralism, whether desirable or not, is an inescapable fact in societies such as ours.[21]

One answer to this is that it assumes that civil society can be sustained only where prior connections exist: might it be, instead, that community has to be achieved? Even the Federation debates did not assume consensus and community, but set about building it. We can see the problems: the construction of community in the 1890s was racist, gendered, class-biased and asserted homogeneity.[22] That is, it was far from perfect, and we may now wish to amend and improve it. But let's remember the practical achievement that Federation was: it did bring together separate colonial populations within an overarching state, but a state that had clear constitutional limits; it did promote economic expansion, but it also provided the framework for ameliorative liberalism; it did provide a ground for defining common interests. The federal movement did tackle each of the elements—the nature of the state, the importance of the economy *and* the type of society to be sustained—that we now see to be important in maintaining the political imagination. As Irving suggests, 'Australia as a nation could not have been achieved without this . . .'[23] This realisation, however, brings us back to the crux of our current problems. Federation was built on the conception of the national community, and the national interest. Fierce current debates about the very idea of the nation may be the most disruptive element in attempts to recover the sense of civil society and community, and yet the citizenship bargain cannot be sustained without these.

Rethinking the nation

The idea of the nation has always been tied to the idea of the citizen. At first, to be a citizen was, formally, to belong to the nation—to have material rights and responsibilities as well as 'imaginary' connections (based on a common history, culture, language, religion and race).[24] As I will show, the problems endemic to imagining links based on shared history, culture and (especially) race should make us recognise that the nation is a political entity. The national idea may mobilise a community. The nation's institutions (such as the constitution) may provide a particular citizenship formula and maintain the sort of civil society we want. But, because these things are the outcome of politics, they are always provisional.

There is an enormous literature on the ideas of 'nation' and 'nationalism'.[25] For our purposes, it is useful to draw out three elements from this discussion. First, while we are encouraged to think of the nation as best symbolising our common interests, and as an organic growth encapsulating our traditions, it has not evolved historically: it is a modern invention. Second, commitment to the nation has had profoundly disparate effects—unifying and mobilising people on the one hand, suppressing 'difference' and causing wars on the other. Third, the nation is said now to be an anachronism, since the purposes it served—identity for particular geo-political communities, maintenance of national boundaries, even self-determination—have been rendered meaningless by the globalising economic institutions of the contemporary world.

Yet we can't turn our backs on the nation, since to do so leaves us blind to the myriad ways in which 'the national' appeal is still used as a means of social control. Not least of these is the way we have been induced to sacrifice real political debate in the face of those economic imperatives said to be in the national interest—a central theme of this book. Not only are ideas of 'the national' still deeply influential in shaping the public culture,[26] but also the identities we are offered and the jurisdictions within which we must live remain nationally bounded. So can we turn 'the nation' to our own purposes?

Nationalism has always been double-edged—an ideology of contest used to inspire and mobilise peoples to fight for their rights and independence, and an ideology which, in the name of common interests, persuades us to subsume differences and abandon sectional demands for the benefit of the community. On the one hand, then, it has been integral to institution building in new societies. On the other, it has ignored ethnic (and, in settler societies like Australia, particularly indigenous) minorities. It has also been deeply gendered, rendering women invisible in debates about the public interest, though their role in nation building is essential.

And of course, as George Orwell, writing in 1945 one of the most brilliant anti-nationalist polemics, 'Notes on nationalism', pointed out, it has fuelled ethnocentrism, hatred, state absolutism and the most destructive wars the world has seen.[27] In short, nationalism has been represented as the essential glue for social cohesion, and as the blight of the modern world.

The contemporary problem in sustaining a positive nationalism is, simply, fragmentation:

> On the one hand technological change, improved
> communications and the growing integration of the world
> market are making the world smaller and more homogeneous;
> on the other hand there is a revived emphasis on difference
> . . . in . . . individual life styles, group cultural identities, or
> assertions of national uniqueness.[28]

We can extend this argument. How can national boundaries be maintained when the flows of people, capital and information are—as we have seen—international, and increasingly so? How can myths of bounded national identities be sustained when cross-cut by immigrant diaspora communities, or when challenged by the demands of indigenous peoples? How can shared mentalities withstand the incursions of a global information superhighway, or of technologies which can deliver through 'narrowcasting' directly to minority audiences? How can a shared national future be voiced when sub-national regions can deal directly with the world?

The nation, on this reading, might be beyond redemption—but we still need community. That is, we need ways of thinking about and identifying our common interests. It's my view, though, that 'the nation' hangs on, not only because of its jurisdictional reality, but also because it remains the best means we have of imagining our common interests. It is, to be sure, an idea which is contingent, historically bounded and will not last for ever—but it may still be a useful tool in the present if we can recover its mobilising potential for proper political ends. And this view seems to be taking hold.

One instance can be found in a feminist criticism of conventional histories of Australia, *Creating a Nation*.[29] There, Patricia Grimshaw and her colleagues argue that, 'National needs, as defined by dominant interests, have often been at variance with the needs and priorities of the different groups that comprise the nation'.[30] Yet, far from giving up on the nation, they conclude that our objective should be the 'reconstruction of the nation . . . the renewal of Australia as a just, fair and heterogeneous society'. The major challenge will be 'to reconcile the imperative towards uniformity . . . with a recognition of the diversity and even incommensurability of the claims emanating from people of different gender, and ethnic, racial, sexual and regional backgrounds'.[31]

Another instance is to be found in Graeme Turner's, *Making It National*, a book concerned with 'Australia's failure to imagine the nation through anything other than discourses (that are) regressive or exclusivist'.[32] 'Australians,' he says, 'have become used to hearing the nation talked about as if it were a brand name, rather than a social community whose interests politics should protect.'[33] And yet, he says, we should not deal with this through dispensing with the category of the nation, but rather by 'a thorough renovation of current defi-nitions . . . so that they more accurately reflect and respond to the interests of all Australian citizens'. The challenge, he continues, is to:

> adapt and transform the discourses of the national to better deal with our current historical circumstances . . . If (a) unifying discourse is to develop . . . it will have to happen through constant negotiation with the kind of critical scrutiny . . . which will enable us to imagine a heterogeneous, hybridized, and socially inclusive Australian society.[34]

Given these problems, how do we proceed to renovation? First, I think, by recognising that not everything that was done in the past was wrong. Consider, again, the example of Fed-eration. It was a process which sought to bring together populations then considerably less homogeneous than they were later to become,[35] and colonies which were by no means persuaded of their common interests. It recognised plurality, and gave this expression through different levels of govern-ment—while arguing for a national interest. While rhetorical use was made of the metaphor of 'the crimson thread of kinship', the work of Federation was achieved through talk, through the adaptation of ideas, through criticism, through negotiation—which is to say, through politics. And of course, there were winners (the urban liberals) and losers (the aspir-ing republicans, but also the Anglo loyalist squattocracy). If the result was biased by the race and gender assumptions common to the times, it was nevertheless a framework that has allowed for continuing political modification (witness, for instance, the 1967 referendum giving Aborigines political rights; the High Court *Mabo* decision allowing native title). This is not to say that the constitution may be changed as readily as we would like, that it has not been a constraint on reformist governments, or even that it is not time for whole-sale revision. It is to say that the real lesson we can take from the 1890s is one of process: the nation we know was not an emanation from history, or from a unified citizenry, but an outcome of borrowed ideas, reflection, talk, publicity, and hard bargaining within a particular set of historical circumstances. It was an outcome of politics.

To accept that the nation is contingent and provisional is to liberate politics. We are not saying, though, that the nation is 'only' provisional—something almost arbitrary that we can shrug off if we so choose. The political decisions of the past have given us material institutions (not least, a constitution) which we would be ill-advised to dismiss lightly. These institutions represent the struggles of peoples who lived together in this land, fought about issues, and 'joined in material and social practices and ordered their affairs in associations and parties'.[36] We should not judge their decisions from our context, nor too hastily assume that we know better.

That said, the nation is not based on sacred tablets, the needs of the present are not always adequately met by decisions that suited a different context in the past, and we are free to change. Politics is the ground where people wrestle with what appears to be 'given' by their past in terms of voicing aspirations and generating choices about the future.

The lesson is that the nation is not beyond politics, it is the sum of politics. It does not emerge 'naturally' out of a homogeneous people united by language or race, but is a political entity born of conflict and compromise. Its core is subjective, a matter of assertion rather than fact. 'National character is what a nation is prepared to talk to itself and others about—it is essentially . . . a conversation piece. It is what citizens are going to talk about in clubs, meeting places and factories.'[37] Community is not the precondition of this conversation, but arises out of it. So do the material things which constitute the citizenship bargain: parliaments, forms of franchise, limits on economic exchange, welfare systems. The conversation will be about balancing priorities, about different values, and about the play of many voices. The solutions achieved will not last (because circumstances will change again), and such commonality as we achieve will need to be capable of continuous revision—a good conversation is never static. But conversation is killed by participants who claim absolute certainty (as do those who cling to the idea of a nation determined by inexorable tradition), or who regard alternative views as unthinkable (which was the position taken by economic rationalists in the recent past). The avoidance of unreflective and manipulative versions of the nation will only be achieved through constant negotiation and critical scrutiny, which brings us back again to the importance of arguments which invoke principles. Seen thus, the nation can again be the means of focusing common interests, providing social cohesion and giving body to the sort of civil society we wish to achieve and to maintain. Eduardo Galeano makes the related point:

> What it all comes down to is that we are the sum of our efforts to change who we are. Identity is no museum piece sitting stock-still in a display case, but rather the endlessly astonishing synthesis of the contradictions of everyday life.[38]

The effort to change who we are will always involve the imaginative elaboration of a better future, and it will always involve politics (the means of negotiating change). A dynamic nation, capable of responding to the many voices of a heterogeneous citizenry and giving body to an achievable civil society, will be the product of political imagination.

Moving on

> There is . . . a time in politics when it is not merely necessary 'to reform in order to preserve' as Burke's great maxim had it, but actually to create in order to preserve.[39]

The ways in which we rethink citizenship, civil society and nation are integral to reviving politics and political imagination. Thinking in terms of civil society encourages us to think of the life of the community beyond state or market. The contemporary debate about civil society reminds us that we can't think of norms in terms of tradition or convention: we must think instead of arguments based on principles. The conception of the nation should not be discarded, for it provides our best means of thinking politically about the processes and institutions necessary to achieve and maintain a particular sort of civil society. Community is not the precondition but the outcome of such activity: community is always in the making. Citizenship, however, is the bottom line: it is where we define the nature of the bargain between individual and nation. Why do such simple arguments have to be made? Because, as this book shows, we are losing the capacity to speak of society in any terms other than the economic. Because, we are told, the nation is a lost cause—outmoded by global capitalism, hopelessly compromised by its past uses, imposing a false unity on our heterogeneity—so we must find a new rhetoric of community (but no one has invented the language). Because we have not seen that citizenship means drawing a line, specifying a bargain, and so have allowed our rights to be leached away by an illiberal market economy. And because, by losing sight of these things, we have lost sight of the purpose of politics, lost the capacity to insist that there are alternative options, lost the means of imagining even how constructive alternatives (such as those outlined in chapter 6) might be deployed. Until we revive politics, such alternatives will hang in the air as mirages.

For all that we now recognise that any useful map of the future will reorient us to civil society, nation and citizenship, when disillusion with politics is at a peak, we may need a mobilising cause to bring things together. What will be the cause of the 1990s?

The turn of centuries, the approach of the millennium, provides the symbolic incentive for substantial reconsideration of the conditions of our culture and politics. Such liminal moments can capture the collective imagination: the 1890s seemed such a time[40]—do the 1990s offer a fresh opportunity? As the centenary of Federation approaches, the constitution that determines our political institutions is being reconsidered. In concert there has been revived attention to the possibility of an Australian republic.

If this was a debate that seemed initially tied to the preoccupations of Paul Keating, it became clear soon after the election of the Coalition government in 1996 that it is a debate that will not go away. Members of the government (such as Senator Baden Teague) have ensured that it remains on the agenda. Howard's supporters announced that his government would move quickly 'to put flesh on the bones' of a constitutional convention process to determine whether Australia would become a republic. Some on both sides of politics insist that it is an idea whose time has come. Others argue that these matters are distractions from the 'real' issues: economic change, social decay, declining infrastructure, globalisation— the familiar litany that has occupied so much space in this book. But it may be that the extensive rethinking of our institutions is the way both to give concrete form to the considerations raised in this chapter, and to address the 'real' issues confronting us. So, I suggest, the republican debate may come to be the cause of the 1990s.

Whatever its origins, whatever partisan associations we have to brush aside, republicanism is a cause that people across the spectrum are beginning to see as one capable of giving concrete form to our rethinking of society, nation and citizenship.

There are six reasons why a wide ranging debate on the Australian republic can give concrete focus to those processes integral to reviving political imagination. First—and perhaps the most familiar argument—such a debate demands a rethinking of how autonomy and independence can be sustained in the current context. It will compel serious reconsideration of what 'the nation' is to mean. The constitutional monarchy remains a link to the colonial past, when we could conceive of sovereignty, but within an empire. Those conditions no longer apply. It's no defence to claim (as even Menzies was wont to do) that the monarchy has no real relevance to our independence. For one thing, the constitutional monarchy muted one of the most powerful rhetorics of modern politics, the rhetoric of citizenship, as we were subjects rather than citizens. Symbolically, sovereignty lay not with the people, but with the crown.[41] For another, it was for too long a buffer against relating directly to the rest of the world (the political equivalent of the 'minatory Englishman', discerned by A.A. Phillips 'in the back of the Australian mind'[42]). But if we shed the sense of someone looking over our shoulders, we are also impelled to think more acutely of just what independence can mean in the 'single world' described by Anthony Giddens.[43] It cannot just be a casting loose, but must raise the question of what exactly is gained by recasting national boundaries in new ways. It involves, in other words, confronting what it is that matters about an Australian geo-political community, what common interest is to be defended, and how that is to be done in the face of insistent globalisation.

Second, the discussion of a republic will stimulate the recovery of a moral language for politics. The normative element has been submerged of late by the instrumental language of economics (politics has been not about what we value, but about what we must do to survive). A revised constitutional framework, however, will impel us to consider the long term, to think about what matters as well as what works, and to what ends. Even the defence of a constitutional monarchy will entail giving voice to what its proponents argue we should value: such arguments will have to be couched in terms of moral principles and logical argument rather than through appeals to tradition.

Third, while sensitising us to the liberating opportunities of change, the republican debate should reacquaint us with some of the strengths of our political heritage. There is a visible republican heritage in the arguments voiced by its historical and contemporary advocates, from John Dunmore Lang and Daniel Deniehy to Geoffrey Dutton and Donald Horne, and we should certainly attend to these. They tell us not about some foreign debate, but about an element embedded within our own political culture. But there is also the covert republicanism of our extant institutions, which is part of their strength: the checks and balances which limit oligarchy in favour of the people's power; the rule of law (such that even Crown immunity from legal suit was long ago abolished); the egalitarian tradition; the infusion of the federal constitution with inherently republican aspects—all those things that have prompted a wide range of scholars[44] to argue that 'if we want to look for republicanism then it is all around us, albeit awaiting consolidation'.[45] In thinking through the possibilities of a republican consolidation, we do not turn our backs on the past, but draw on elements of the habits and practices some would claim are most distinctively Australian.

Fourth, the historical embeddedness of Australian republicanism makes it feasible to argue, as has Philip Pettit, that 'we are heirs to a common set of ideas', that 'can provide a shared perspective on change, agreed terms of reference, and a common language for articulating what is and should be happening'.[46] Why is the old language of 'the Australian settlement' no longer feasible as such a common language? Because it is not a language of autonomy, or of rights, or of relevance to the non-Anglo immigrant community for whom monarchy is not salient. And it is irretrievably implicated in the politics of race, gender, class and (oppressive) unity historically associated with nationalism. Republicanism, as argued above, enables us to draw on those aspects of the past not implicated in that sort of nationalism.

To argue that there are elements of a common language is a bold step in the face of influential theories (following Levi Strauss, Derrida, Foucault, Kristeva, Irigaray) that suggest little possibility of communicating across difference.[47] To take this step demands an element of faith, in the possibilities of politics, and of conversation. We might accept that languages are relative; that key terms (like, say, 'justice') are relative to the play of power—and are usually defined by elites in terms which justify their power; and that there are therefore grounds for being suspicious of all universalising statements. But should we take this to mean that there is no way of talking of, say, 'justice' in a collective sense? I think politics depends on an acceptance that, in everyday life, there is an acceptance of what 'justice' means without widespread misunderstanding, that is neither eternal nor universal, but that can be the basis for political action.[48] We can see hegemonic language at work (for instance, in the widespread notion of the past decade of justice as individual, delivered by markets, based on access to property), but we can also see that the hegemonic language never 'takes' perfectly, that dissenting voices draw both on past notions of justice (as, say, connected with welfare), and on different perspectives of the present, to reconstitute an 'everyday' sense of fairness.

Fifth, republicanism, because it involves thinking of how to articulate the hierarchy of citizen rights, may offer a common language capable of accommodating the 'politics of difference'.[49] The feminist debate on republicanism starts to make this clear.[50] It does not, for one thing, have to be a 'boys own' republic. The insistence on difference has been an important tactic in drawing attention to gender issues, but in its wake there had to be a recognition that there are many different axes of oppression (and, indeed, many feminisms). Thus, 'not only do . . . various emancipatory movements have to accept each other's presence, but they have to work with this presence as part of their *internal* politics'.[51] Emancipatory movements might each have distinctive claims against the status quo, but should recognise something in common in respect of their claims on justice, which brings me back to the argument above for an everyday sense of fairness. With respect to current feminist discussions of republicanism, we might accept that conventional masculine demands reflect concerns for individual independence (safeguards against the state), while women are 'more concerned about rape, domestic violence, incest, poverty and childcare'[52] (and protection against these). An unambiguous resolution—say, a bill of rights—is unlikely to ameliorate such conflict. But a republican framework that recognises the need for continuous negotiation (that is to say, an ongoing politics) between political rights (independence, freedom, equality), civil rights (guarantees of protection) and social rights (access to the means of ensuring basic equity in life chances) could accommodate the politics of difference, not just in relation to gender, but to race, and class as well. At base, this encourages the recognition that for all our manifold differences, there are areas of overlap on issues like equality and justice, that these are the grounds of citizenship, and that a republican framework can provide the means for the political mediation of a general interest on these grounds.

Sixth, the republican debate, in bringing to the surface the question of rights, and hence the bargain between citizen and state (that is, of exactly what inclusion as a citizen within the republic entails), ultimately raises the question of what we want democracy to mean. If it is to mean some power over the circumstances that govern our lives, it will mean not only a voice in governance, but an insistence that politics should be able to override the unwanted effects of the free market and the 'single world'. Republican institutions will have to be designed with that in mind. As Philip Pettit and others argue,[53] republicanism is in some respects against the tradition of individualistic liberalism that has left us without resources in asserting a general interest as a constraint on free markets.

> The liberal attachment to the market . . . has made the image of voter as consumer a very beguiling one. By contrast, the dominant theme in republican writing is that voting is important because in voting, people are recruited to the business of government, forming and expressing their considered view as to what is for the public good . . . [54]

Liberalism, ideally, is isolationist: 'to be perfectly free is to lack the interference of others in your life and affairs, to live without restraint'. Republicanism, in contrast, is distinctively communal: 'the image of perfect freedom . . . is that of enjoying the freedom of the city: the status of being fully enfranchised, fully incorporated in the body politic'.[55] A community whose highest ideal is the maximisation of self-interest will inevitably see the sort of attrition of politics I have described in this book. A community which adopts measures through which the 'people are recruited to the business of government', and in which people are 'fully incorporated in the body politic', will be one in which the political imagination thrives. My argument is that such a community will be achieved through the consolidation of an Australian republic.

For all that, the republican debate may go off the boil for any number of reasons, not least, a failure of the imaginative leadership that can connect the public need for a new sense of direction with this civic exercise.

Voices and leaders

A simplistic view of democracy has it that generalising ideas arise from the people. It is more accurate to say that modern societies have created groups who specialise in producing, debating and disseminating ideas: we loosely describe them as the intelligentsia[56] (writers, journalists, artists, teachers, academics—and when it comes to politics, speech-writers and policy advisers), and their story is introduced in chapter 5. For their ideas to bear fruit requires a relationship between intellectuals (broadly defined) and politicians. Ideas may reach the public domain in many ways, but it is usually when leaders make them an issue that they mobilise interests and become part of political debate. (Remember Paul Keating's skill with the 'spray can', sketching big pictures that then remain on the public agenda—see chapter 5.) The democratic moment comes when we make informed choices about the options presented to us.

The political culture is, in a sense, produced by the relations between leaders and the intelligentsia. Political action always calls for justification, and the legitimating patterns of ideas are produced by the intelligentsia.[57] Their messages call on particular views of Australia or Australian interests, designed to persuade an audience to accept a specific course of action. Thus the political culture is reinterpreted as competing intellectuals stir the pot, giving new twists to 'traditions', feeding in contemporary theories from transnational intellectual networks and adding initiatives appropriate to their context. These messages are taken up by political activists to legitimise particular political programs.

This sort of symbiosis is inescapable. At its best, it provides much that is valuable in our collective life: putting problems into words, identifying potential solutions, producing messages that inspire and mobilise. But it can also give rise to the pathology I've described as the betrayal of the intelligentsia in chapter 5. This happens when leaders listen only to their advisers (when, that is, political elites talk only to each other); when the needs of the community slip from sight (and the needs of the economy become overriding); when every political problem is deemed capable of a technical solution; when 'specialists' lose the capacity to translate their preoccupations into modes intelligible to the rest of us; when the 'national conversation' at the heart of politics breaks down.

A lively intellectual culture demands 'critics' as well as 'experts': the former will emerge from training institutions which promote free enquiry rather than those bludgeoned into accordance with the 'national priorities' of the day.[58] Options, alternatives and dispute within mainstream politics are more likely to be promoted where the participating intelligentsia come from many backgrounds rather than when there is an overwhelming dominance of one discipline or one intellectual world view, such as Michael Pusey found in Canberra.[59] We would do well, therefore, to monitor the complexion of the public service and the recruitment of advisers. Is it too optimistic to expect that the relations between the bearers of ideas and their political masters should be transparent? (Studies of Chifley, Whitlam and Fraser, for instance, show pretty clearly who fed in ideas and with what effects.[60]) At the least we should demand that both our leaders and our intellectuals address us in the common language—promoting real conversation—rather than passing down unintelligible nostrums which claim the authority of expertise. Proper interrogation of alternatives will be enhanced by parliaments with their own access to intellectual resources, and the means to assert views against executive government: enhancement of parliamentary members' staff and the elaboration of committee systems are moves in this direction. Public debate will be fostered by concerted scrutiny through the media. This will not happen while the media are populated by people whose views are identical to those of the politicians and advisers they report.[61] And it will not happen where the personalisation of combat politics and the theatre of economics substitute for the analysis of ideas. There is unlikely to be wide-ranging and diverse debate where media monopolies dominate the field, and the concentration of media ownership in Australia is therefore a continuing concern.[62] We must demand better.

Above all, we must recognise that the relations between leaders and the bearers of ideas are functional, contingent on context, pragmatic, and lead to provisory outcomes at best. Such a recognition protects us from the delusion that the solutions of the moment are 'natural' or 'inevitable', and hence above politics. The limit of politics is that it does not arrive at answers for all time, which is to say the 'end of history' is a false ideal. The beauty of politics is that it can liberate us from the dead hand of the past and the false starts of the present. As long as we keep asking questions.

Notes

Introduction   A defence of politics

1   *Australian*, 22 July 1994.
2   Hugh Mackay, *Reinventing Australia: The mind and mood of Australia in the 90s*, Angus & Robertson, Sydney, 1993, pp.167–84.
3   Mackay, *Reinventing Australia*, p.175.
4   Paul Kelly, *The End of Certainty: The story of the 1980s*, Allen & Unwin, Sydney, 1992, p.686.
5   See, for instance, Graham Little, *Political Ensembles: A psychosocial approach to politics and leadership*, Oxford University Press, Melbourne, 1985, especially chapter 8; and James David Barber, *The Pulse of Politics: Electing presidents in the media age*, WW Norton, New York, 1980, chapters 1 and 2.
6   Bernard Crick, *In Defence of Politics*, Penguin, London, [1962] 1992. I have chosen deliberately to reflect Crick's title in the heading to this introduction.
7   Aristotle, quoted in Crick, *In Defence of Politics*, p.161. And see pp.17–18.
8   Crick, *In Defence of Politics*, p.25.
9   Edward Said, *Representations of the Intellectual: The 1993 Reith Lectures*, Vintage, London, 1994, especially chapter 5.
10 Benedict Anderson, *Imagined Communities: Reflections on the origin and spread of nationalism*, Verso, London, 1983.
11 I argue this point at greater length in 'From the *Weird Mob* to *Strictly Ballroom*: politics and public culture in Australia since the forties', plenary address to the British Australian Studies Association biennial conference, University of Kent, 2 September 1994, and forthcoming in *Australian Studies* (UK).

12 Paul Keating, 'Politics: contest between pragmatists and posturers', *The Canberra Times*, 8 August 1994, p.9 (and see also that paper's editorial for that day).

13 Michael Pusey, *Economic rationalism in Canberra: A nation-building state changes its mind*, Cambridge University Press, Sydney, 1991.

14 Hugh Emy, *Remaking Australia: The state, the market and Australia's future*, Allen & Unwin, Sydney, 1993.

15 For Manning Clark's view, see his *A History of Australia, Volume V: The people make laws 1888–1915*, Melbourne University Press, Melbourne, 1981, chapters 5 and 6, and for a sketch of the revisionist view, see Helen Irving, 'Who were the republicans?' in D Headon, J Warden and B Gammage, eds, *Crown or Country: The traditions of Australian republicanism*, Allen & Unwin, Sydney, 1994, pp.69–82. For further discussion, see chapter 7 below.

16 Frances Fukuyama, *The End of History and the Last Man*, Penguin, London, 1992.

17 Kelly, *The End of Certainty*

18 James Walter, 'The failure of political imagination', *Australian Quarterly*, vol. 65, no. 1, 1993, pp.546–57.

Chapter 1 Frontier stories

1 Bob Hawke, speaking on 'Labor in Power', ABC-TV, June 1993. The comment is repeated, unchanged, in *The Hawke Memoirs*, Heinemann, Port Melbourne, 1994, p.175.

2 *One Nation*, Statement by the Prime Minister, The Honourable PJ Keating, MP. 26 February 1992, AGPS, Canberra, 1992, p.9.

3 Edmund Barton, *Sydney Morning Herald*, 1 January 1901. Quoted in FK Crowley, ed., *Modern Australia in Documents, vol.1, 1901–1939*, Wren, Melbourne, 1973, pp.4–5.

4 Sir Otto Niemeyer, *Sydney Morning Herald*, 22 August 1930. Quoted in WF Mandle, *Going It Alone: Australia's national identity in the twentieth century*, Penguin, Richmond, 1980, pp.79–80.

5 Sylvia Lawson, *The Archibald Paradox*, Allen Lane, Ringwood, 1983, p.ix.

6 Andrew Gliniecki, 'Paris overtakes London for ease of commuting', *The Independent*, 6 June 1992.

7 London Planning Advisory Committee, *London: World city*, HMSO, London, 1991, p.130.

8 LPAC, *London: World city*, p.130.

9 My views on these issues were formed largely by reading the *Financial Times* regularly in the period 1990–1993. But discussion with Hugo Hinsley in London undoubtedly added focus: see also Hinsley, 'Docklands is not the only future', in J Walter, H Hinsley and P Spearritt, eds, *Changing Cities: Reflections on Britain and Aus-*

tralia, Sir Robert Menzies Centre for Australian Studies, London, 1995, pp. 67–83.

10 Quoted in, 'The president steps back through the looking glass', *Australian*, 14 January 1994, p.6.

Chapter 2   Transforming the Australian public culture

1 T B Millar, *Australia in Peace and War*, second edition, Australian National University Press, Canberra, 1991, chapter 21.

2 Bob Hawke 'Australia's security in Asia: the strategic relationship', *Australian Foreign Affairs and Trade: The monthly record*, vol. 62, no. 9, May 1991, p.199.

3 Gareth Evans, 'Australia is catching up with its geography', *Australian Foreign Affairs and Trade: The monthly record*, vol. 61, no. 7, July 1990, p.421.

4 Gareth Evans, 'The Asia–Pacific and global change', *Australian Foreign Affairs and Trade: The monthly record*, vol. 62, no. 4, April 1991, p.126.

5 The phrase is Benedict Anderson's—see his essential book on nationalism, *Imagined Communities*, Verso, London, 1983.

6 Ross Garnaut, *Australia and the Northeast Asian Ascendancy*, AGPS, Canberra, 1989.

7 See the 6 articles debating Garnaut's argument, and Garnaut's response, in *Australian Journal of International Affairs*, vol. 44, no. 1, April 1990.

8 John McKay, 'Australia and the northeast Asian ascendancy: Some commentaries on the Garnaut Report', *Australian Journal of International Affairs*, vol. 44, no. 1, April 1990, p.1.

9 Evans, 'Australia is catching up with its geography', p.424.

10 Evans, 'The Asia–Pacific and global change', p.125.

11 Greg Sheridan, 'The leap to free trade', *Australian*, November 14, 1994. Sheridan is an enthusiastic proselyte for APEC.

12 Richard Woolcott (Secretary of the Department of Foreign Affairs and Trade), 'Asia–Pacific: Australia's challenge for the '90s', *Australian Foreign Affairs and Trade: The monthly record*, vol. 62. no. 1, September 1991, pp.554–5.

13 Though Evans, on occasion, conceded that the picture is more complicated: see note 22 below.

14 For a clear statement in this vein, see Woolcott, 'Asia–Pacific: Australia's challenge for the '90s', p.555.

15 Evans, 'The Asia–Pacific and global change', p.126.

16 Woolcott, 'Asia–Pacific...', p.557

17 Rawdon Dalrymple, 'Is Australia a part of Asia?' *Australian Foreign Affairs and Trade: The monthly record*, vol. 61, no. 10, October 1990, p.719.

18 Evans, 'The Asia–Pacific and global change', p.126.
19 D A Low, 'Australia in the eastern hemisphere', *Australian Studies* (UK), no. 4, December 1990, pp.60–76, p.67.
20 Low, 'Australia in the eastern hemisphere', pp.67–8.
21 See, especially, Edward Said, *Orientalism*, Pantheon, New York, 1978.
22 Evans, 'Australia is catching up with its geography', p.425.
23 Evans, 'Australia is catching up with its geography', p.425
24 This is the principal claim made about the Australian mindset in politics in Peter Loveday's 'Australian political thought' in R Lucy, ed., *The Pieces of Politics*, second edition, Macmillan, Melbourne, 1975, pp.2–28. See also Donald Denoon, *Settler capitalism*, Oxford University Press, New York, 1983.
25 See the statement of a L–NCP Minister for Foreign Affairs, Tony Street, in Low, 'Australia in the eastern hemisphere', p.67.
26 See James Walter, *The Leader: a political biography of Gough Whitlam*, University of Queensland Press, St Lucia, 1980, pp.117–26.
27 John Docker, *The Nervous Nineties: Australian cultural life in the 1890s*, Oxford University Press, Melbourne, 1991, chapters 18 and 19; and John Docker, *Dilemmas of Identity: The desire for the other in colonial and post colonial cultural history*, Working Paper No. 74, SRMCAS, London, 1991.
28 Annette Hamilton, 'Fear and desire: Aborigines, Asians and the national imaginary' *Australian Cultural History*, no. 9, 1990, pp.14–35.
29 See Nicholas Brown, 'Australian intellectuals and the image of Asia, 1920–1960', *Australian Cultural History*, no. 9, 1990, pp.80–92; David Walker and John Ingleson, 'The impact of Asia', in Neville Meaney, ed., *Under New Heavens*, Heinemann, Melbourne, 1989, pp.287–324.
30 D Walker and J Ingleson, 'The impact of Asia', pp.300–303.
31 D Walker and J Ingleson, 'The impact of Asia', p.290.
32 Docker, *Dilemmas of Identity*, pp.13–17.
33 On Latham, see Stuart Macintyre's entry in *Australian Dictionary of Biography*, vol.10 Melbourne University Press, Melbourne, 1986, pp.2–6; Clune's novel is discussed by Walker and Ingleson, 'The impact of Asia', p.313; the rest of this list paraphrases Brown, 'Australian intellectuals and the image of Asia', pp.81–85.
34 Cited in Walker and Ingleson, 'The impact of Asia', p.315.
35 Humphrey McQueen, in his provocative article about Australia's place in an empire economy, 'The suckling society' in H Mayer and H Nelson, eds, *Australian Politics—A third reader*, Cheshire, Melbourne, 1973, pp.5–13.
36 See Denoon, *Settler Capitalism*.
37 Carl Bridge, 'Poland to Pearl Harbour', in his edited volume, *Munich to Vietnam: Australia's relations with Britain and the United States since the 1930s*, Melbourne University Press, Melbourne, 1991, pp.38–51, p.39.
38 Bridge, 'Poland to Pearl Harbour', p.40.
39 Bridge, 'Poland to Pearl Harbour', p.195.

40 See Carl Bridge, *'Special Relationships': Australia, Britain and the United States since 1941*, Trevor Reese Memorial Lecture, SRMCAS, London, 1991, pp.18–19; and compare Low, 'Australia in the eastern hemisphere', pp.69–76.

41 Bridge, *'Special Relationships'*..., p.10.

42 This is a particular case in a specific policy area of the general process described by Richard White in his *Inventing Australia*, Allen & Unwin, Sydney, 1981.

43 I am borrowing here from the closing argument of C Bridge, *Munich to Vietnam*, p.196—though with somewhat different emphasis.

Chapter 3   The message from 'the great elsewhere'

1 Francis Fukuyama, 'The end of history', *Quadrant*, vol.34, no.8, August 1989, pp.15–25. The article was first published in the US journal, *The National Interest*, no.16, Summer 1989, pp.3–18, and then energetically promoted by that journal's (Australian) editor, Owen Harries, and republished around the world.

2 Francis Fukuyama, *The End of History and the Last Man*, Penguin, London, 1992.

3 Evans, 'The Asia-Pacific and global change', p.129.

4 Fukuyama, 'End of history', p.15.

5 Fukuyama, 'End of history', p.16.

6 Fukuyama, 'End of history', p.19.

7 Fukuyama, 'End of history', p.22.

8 Fukuyama, 'End of history', p.22.

9 Fukuyama, 'End of history', p.22.

10 Fukuyama, *End of History and the Last Man*, p.92.

11 Fukuyama, *End of History and the Last Man*, p.108.

12 Fukuyama, 'End of history', p.17.

13 Fukuyama, 'End of history', p.19.

14 Fukuyama, 'End of history', p.21.

15 Fukuyama, 'End of history', p.23 and pp.24–5.

16 Paul Kelly, *The End of Certainty: The story of the 1980s*, Allen & Unwin, Sydney, 1992.

17 Kelly, *End of Certainty*, chapter 1.

18 WK Hancock, *Australia*, Ernest Benn, London, 1930, chapters 5 and 7; FW Eggleston, *State Socialism in Victoria*, P.S. King & Sons, London, 1932.

19 Kelly, *End of Certainty*, p.668.

20 Kelly, *End of Certainty*, p.666.

21 Kelly, *End of Certainty*, p.683.

22 Kelly, *End of Certainty*, pp.14–15.

23 Kelly, *End of Certainty*, p.680.

24 Kelly, *End of Certainty*, p.670.

25 Alan Wood's articles are, 'Oiling the global machinery', 'US and Japan: The troubled titans' and 'No turning back' and they appear in *Australian* on 8, 10 and 11 January 1994 respectively.

26 Terry McCrann, 'Capitalism to the rescue and no losers', *Australian*, 2 October 1993.

27 Kelly, *End of Certainty*, p.682.

Chapter 4 Problems with the message

1 Fukuyama refers indirectly to ameliorative liberalism in conceding that most modern liberal democracies entail an active public sector and the acceptance of responsibility for social welfare, but the force of his rhetoric and argument is unmistakably with the tremendous homogenising power of, and the creation of parallel aspirations by, the international free market. See *The End of History and the Last Man*, chapter 9, and compare, especially, p.44, p.290 and p.108.

2 On ameliorative liberalism, see Peter Tiver, *The Liberal Party: Principles and performance*, Jacaranda, Brisbane, 1978, chapter 2; Bill Brugger and Dean Jaensch, *Australian Politics: Theory and practice*, Allen & Unwin, Sydney, 1985, chapters 1 and 2.

3 For an overview see Brian Head, ed., *State and Economy in Australia*, Oxford University Press, Melbourne, 1983.

4 Kelly, *End of Certainty*, p.7.

5 Peter Cochrane, *Industrialization and Dependence: Australia's road to economic development*, University of Queensland Press, St Lucia, 1980. The rest of this paragraph closely paraphrases Cochrane's overview in chapter 1.

6 This was the 'men, money, markets' scheme—see Kosmas Tsokhas, *Markets, Money and Empire*, Oxford University Press, Melbourne, 1990.

7 Cochrane, *Industrialization and Dependence*, p.13.

8 RW Connell and TH Irving, *Class Structure in Australian History*, Longman Cheshire, Melbourne, 1980, p.294.

9 Tsokhas, *Markets, Money and Empire*.

10 Bridge, *Special Relationships*, p.10.

11 See Colin White, *Mastering Risk: Environment, markets and politics in Australian economic history*, Oxford University Press, Melbourne, 1992. This is also a central element in Michael Pusey's *Economic Rationalism in Canberra* which I discuss further in chapter 5, below.

12 See Immanuel Wallerstein, *Geopolitics and Geoculture: Essays on the changing world system*, Cambridge University Press, Cambridge, 1991, p.124. The paragraph as a whole draws heavily on Wallerstein, chapters 3 and 9.

13 David Harvey, *The Condition of Postmodernity*, Blackwell, Oxford, 1989, p.145.

14 Harvey, *The Condition of Postmodernity*, p.160.
15 Harvey, *The Condition of Postmodernity*, p.163.
16 Harvey, *The Condition of Postmodernity*, pp.164–5.
17 Anthony Giddens, *Modernity and Self-identity*, Polity Press, Cambridge, 1991, p.27.
18 See, for instance, John Carroll and Robert Manne, eds, *Shutdown: The failure of economic rationalism and how to rescue Australia*, Text Publishing, Melbourne, 1992; Boris Frankel, *From the Prophets Deserts Come*, Arena Publishing, Melbourne, 1992; Pusey, *Economic Rationalism in Canberra*.
19 Robert Kuttner, 'Brave new world in the workplace', *Guardian Weekly*, 8 August 1993; Martin Woollacott, 'Jobs must be made a protected species', *Guardian Weekly*, 22 August 1993.
20 This paragraph condenses material cited in Will Hutton, 'Crime, the politicians' rich reward', *The Guardian*, 4 July 1992, and on 'The Big Picture' program on crime, Channel 4 (UK), 4 July 1992. See also Will Hutton, 'A society that cries shame on Britain', *Guardian Weekly*, 25 July 1993.
21 For an early, and prescient critique, see Hugh Stretton, 'Privatizing and deregulating the mixed economy', in his *Political Essays*, Georgian House, Melbourne, 1987, pp.23–53.
22 See Katrina Alford, 'Econotalk: The case of financial deregulation', *Meanjin*, vol. 51, no.4, 1992, pp.766–784.
23 Rebecca Smithers, 'Rail privatisation to cost £200m', and editorial 'Running late and out of date', *Guardian Weekly*, 15 August 1993.
24 John Docker, 'Popular culture versus the state: An argument against Australian content regulations for television', *Media Information Australia*, no.59, February 1991, pp.7–26.
25 See, for instance, Leicester Webb, 'The social control of television', *Public Administration* (Sydney), September 1960, pp.193–214.
26 Jennifer Craik, 'Popular, commercial and national imperatives of australian broadcasting', *Media Information Australia*, no.59, February 1991, p.35.
27 Docker, 'Popular culture versus the state', p.24.
28 Raymond Williams, 'Cinema and socialism', in his *The Politics of Modernism*, ed., Tony Pinkney, Verso, London, 1989, p.110.
29 Quoted in 'Why the Gatt trade talks must succeed', *Guardian Weekly*, 17 October 1993, p.22.
30 See 'Trade: The new world order', *Australian*, 16 December 1993, p.29.
31 These points are forcefully made by Kevin Watkins, 'Trade package will only make the poor poorer', *Guardian Weekly*, 26 December 1993, p.6.
32 Watkins, 'Trade package will only make the poor poorer'.
33 'Trade: The new world order', *Australian*, 16 December 1993; 'Gatt: who wins what?' *Guardian Weekly*, 26 December 1993, p.6.

34 Terry McCrann, 'Capitalism to the rescue and no losers', *Australian*, 2 October 1993.
35 Gustavo Esteva, cited in Wolfgang Sachs, ed., *The Development Dictionary: a guide to knowledge as power*, Zed Books, London, 1992.
36 Helena Norberg-Hodge, *Ancient Futures: Learning from Ladakh*, Rider, London, 1992.
37 Lena Sun, 'Capitalism puts China's workers on their knees', *Guardian Weekly*, 28 November 1993, p.17; Christopher Thomas, 'Economic reforms worsen plight of India's poor', *Australian*, 7 March 1995.
38 James Goldsmith, 'Economic disaster called GATT', *Guardian Weekly*, October 16, 1994.
39 Fukuyama, 'End of history', pp.24–5.

Chapter 5   The failure of political imagination

1 See Carroll and Manne, eds, *Shutdown*, for a collection of essays from right and left on this theme.
2 For more extended discussion of these comparisons, see my 'The failure of political imagination'. And for comprehensive analysis of the Australian 1993 federal elections, see 'Special issue—Election '93', *Australian Journal of Political Science*, vol. 29, 1994.
3 See e.g. Paul Kelly, *The Hawke Ascendancy*, Angus & Robertson, Sydney, 1984; Kelly, *End of Certainty*, Part 1, 'The revolution begins'; Dean Jaensch, *The Hawke–Keating Hijack: the ALP in transition*, Allen & Unwin, Sydney, 1989.
4 RG Menzies, 'The forgotten people', in *The Liberal Party of Australia: A documentary history*, ed. Graeme Starr, Drummond/Heinemann, Richmond, 1980, pp.57–63; and see Judith Brett's extended analysis in her *Robert Menzies Forgotten People*, Part 1. See also Ian Cook, 'From Menzies to Hewson' in Geoff Stokes, ed., *Australian Political Ideas*, UNSW Press, Kensington, 1994, pp.168–95.
5 Gough Whitlam, 'The road to reform—Labor in government', in his *On Australia's Constitution*, Widescope, Melbourne, 1977, p.210.
6 Patrick Weller, *Malcolm Fraser PM*, Penguin, Ringwood, 1989.
7 Malcolm Fraser, 'Our economic ailments subject to misdiagnosis', *Australian*, 19 January 1994.
8 Menzies, 'Forgotten people'; Ben Chifley, 'The light on the hill', in *A Documentary History of the Australian Labor Movement 1850–1975*, ed. Brian McKinlay, Drummond, Richmond, 1979, pp.186–87; Whitlam, *On Australia's Constitution*; *Malcolm Fraser on Australia*, (eds DM White & DA Kemp), Hill of Content, Melbourne, 1986.
9 RJL Hawke, *The Resolution of Conflict, 1979 Boyer Lectures*, Australian Broadcasting Commission, Sydney, 1979.
10 Stan Anson, *Hawke: An emotional life*, McPhee Gribble, Ringwood, 1991, chapter 4.

11 Stephen Mills, *The Hawke Years: The story from the inside*, Viking, Ringwood, 1993, p.300.

12 Mills, *The Hawke Years: The story from the inside*, p.100, p.102.

13 Quoted in Mills, *The Hawke Years: The story from the inside*, p.71.

14 Bob Hawke, *The Hawke Memoirs*, Heinemann, Port Melbourne, 1994, p.98.

15 Hawke, *Memoirs*, pp.1–30.

16 Hawke's *Memoirs*, despite a denial on p.164, make this evident, see p.161, p.184, pp.498–500. See also Anson, *Hawke*, chapter 3.

17 'The Talkshow', SBS–TV, 14 February 1994.

18 See e.g. Graham Little, 'Inside the mind of Keating', *Herald–Sun* (Melbourne), 27 February 1993.

19 'The Talkshow', SBS–TV, 14 February 1994; ABC–TV, 'Labor in Power', five episodes: 8 June, 15 June, 22 June, 29 June, and 6 July 1993.

20 Walter, *The Leader: A political biography of Gough Whitlam*, p.247.

21 Quoted in Bruce Loudon, 'Paul Keating', *Herald–Sun* (Melbourne), 27 February 1993.

22 Fia Cumming, *Mates: Five champions of the Labor Right*, Allen & Unwin, Sydney, 1991; direct quotes on Lang from 'The Talkshow', SBS–TV, 14 February 1994; and from John Murphy, 'The Labors of Keating', *Arena Magazine*, no.6, August–September 1993, p.20.

23 'The Talkshow', SBS–TV, 14 February 1994.

24 'The Talkshow'.

25 Edna Carew, *Keating: A biography*, Allen & Unwin, Sydney, 1988, chapters 1 and 2.

26 Little, 'Inside the mind of Keating'; Michael Gordon, *A Question of Leadership: Paul Keating political fighter*, UQP, St Lucia, 1993.

27 See Graham Freudenberg, *A Certain Grandeur: Gough Whitlam in politics*, Macmillan, Melbourne, 1977; Walter, *The Leader*.

28 'The Talkshow'.

29 'Labor in Power'—ABC Television, broadcast in 5 episodes during June–July 1993 (see note 19 above). All direct quotations in the discussion below are from these telecasts.

30 David Morgan, 'Labor in Power'.

31 See Greg Whitwell, *The Treasury Line*, Allen & Unwin, Sydney, 1986.

32 'Victory from true believers', *Australian*, 15 March 1993.

33 John Murphy, 'The Labors of Keating', *Arena Magazine*, no.6, August–September 1993, pp.18–20.

34 *Working Nation—White Paper on Employment and Growth*, AGPS, Canberra, 1994, and see Keating's 'A blueprint for the time we live in', *Australian*, 5 May 1994; *Creative Nation: Commonwealth Cultural Policy October 1994*, Commonwealth of Australia, Canberra, 1994; Paul Keating's second reading speech on the introduction of the *Native Title Bill 1993*, CPD, vol.190, pp.2877–83 (16 November 1993); 'Whereas the people...': Civics and Citizenship Education, Report of the Civics Expert Group, AGPS, Canberra, 1994; reports on the 'National

Strategies Conference' appeared in all metropolitan newspapers on 26 November 1994.

35 See, for instance, 'Libs without policy on republic: PM', *Australian*, 12 July 1994; 'Sensitive new-age Keating?' *Australian*, 10 October 1994.

36 Speech by the Prime Minister, the Hon. PJ Keating MP, University of Melbourne Graduate School, Inaugural Dean's Lecture, 5 August 1994.

37 James Jupp and Marian Sawer, 'Building coalitions: The Australian Labor Party and the 1993 general election', *Australian Journal of Political Science*, vol. 29, Special Issue, 1993, pp.10–27.

38 For citations for Menzies, Whitlam and Fraser, see note 8 above.

39 'The Talkshow', SBS–TV, 14 February 1994.

40 Donald Horne, 'Cultural blindness blurs vision', *Sydney Morning Herald*, 24 October 1994.

41 *One Nation*, Statement by the Prime Minister, The Honourable PJ Keating, MP, 26 February 1992, AGPS, Canberra.

42 See, for instance, Alan Wood, 'Fightback vs One Nation', *Australian*, 14 March 1992, p.19.

43 See Hugh Emy, *Remaking Australia*, pp.161–3.

44 John Langmore and John Quiggin, *Work for All: Full employment in the nineties*, Melbourne University Press, Melbourne, 1994.

45 Horne, 'Cultural blindness blurs vision'.

46 Speech by the Prime Minister, The Hon. PJ Keating MP, Asia Lecture to the Asia–Australia Institute, Brisbane, 26 October 1994, p.12.

47 Professor Fred Hilmer's report on competition policy—designed to expose government utilities and agencies to the disciplines of market competition—was released in late 1993, supported by the federal government and persistently debated for over a year before resolution. The sticking point was insistence by the States on fiscal compensation for abandoning their monopolies.

48 Enthusiastic support for Keating's efforts on APEC has been the tenor of newspaper commentary—see the metropolitan newspaper reports of the APEC leaders meeting in November 1994 (12–18 November 1994) for instance. For Keating's own account of the centrality of APEC, see Paul Keating, 'Our nation's future lies in liberalising the market', *Australian*, 14 November 1994; and his 'Asia–Australia Institute Speech' (above), pp.8–10.

49 Fukuyama, *End of History and the Last Man*, p.311.

50 *Future Directions: It's time for plain thinking*, Liberal and National Parties, December 1988.

51 *Fightback! Taxation and expenditure reform for jobs and growth*, Liberal Party of Australia, Melbourne, 1991.

52 Emy, *Remaking Australia*, p.111. The following account draws extensively on Emy's careful exposition.

53 *Fightback! It's your Australia*, Liberal and National Parties, Canberra, 1991, p.23 and p.36.

54 Emy, *Remaking Australia*, p.111.

55 Emy, *Remaking Australia*, p.114.

56 Judith Brett, 'What ever happened to moral purpose?', *Age*, 27 February 1993; 'Libs lose track of the forgotten people', *Australian*, 17 March 1993; and *Liberal Philosophy from Menzies to Hewson*, Paper given to Australian Political Science Association conference, Monash University, 1 October 1993. This paragraph draws on the latter.

57 Brett, *Liberal Philosophy from Menzies to Hewson*, p.4.

58 Brett, *Liberal Philosophy from Menzies to Hewson*, p.8.

59 Kelly, *End of Certainty*, p.614.

60 John Gray, 'Against the new liberalism', *Times Literary Supplement*, 3 July 1992; Ferdinand Mount, 'Free market fails to deliver the goods', *Australian*, 26 January 1994 and 'Righting the wrongs of modern existence', *Australian*, 2 February 1994.

61 *Australian*, 24 May 1994.

62 See e.g. Mike Steketee, 'A Party in need of a future', *Australian*, 21–22 May 1994.

63 Peter Costello, 'Four fundamentals of the Liberal way', *Australian*, 18 May 1994.

64 Lenore Taylor, 'Downer's battle plan', *Australian*, 3 June 1994.

65 In 1989 he had said on the question of an eventual return to leadership, 'That (would be) Lazarus with a triple by-pass'. For both comments, see *Australian*, 26 January 1995.

66 Career details are covered in many articles discussing Howard's renaissance; see, for instance, Mike Steketee, 'John Howard's second coming', *Australian*, 21–22 January 1995.

67 I combine two passages from Rod Cameron here—the first quoted in Laura Tingle, 'Liberals march to voters with battle-weary troops', *Australian*, 26 January 1995; and the second in Michael Gordon, 'Out of the ashes', *Australian*, 28–29 January 1995.

68 John Howard quoted in 'Succession marks "the return of an alternative" ', *Australian*, 31 January 1995.

69 Henderson is quoted in Greg Lindsay, 'Libs will sink or swim in policy think-tank', *Australian*, 31 October 1994.

70 Laura Tingle, 'Liberals march to voters with battle-weary troops', *Australian*, 26 January 1995.

71 See Walter, *The Ministers' Minders*; and in addition see this author's *States of Mind: Intellectuals and political culture in Australia and Britain*, Sir Robert Menzies Centre for Australian Studies, London, 1990; 'Prime ministers and their staff', in *Menzies to Keating: The development of the Australian prime ministership*, ed. P Weller, Melbourne University Press, Melbourne, 1992, pp.28–63; and 'Intellectuals', in *Australian Civilization*, ed. R Nile, Oxford University Press, Melbourne, 1994, pp.162–79.

72 The proponents of Keynesian reconstruction in the 1940s, for instance: see HC Coombs, *Trial Balance: Issues of my working life*, Macmillan, Melbourne, 1981, p.6.

73 Walter, *The Ministers' Minders*; and 'Prime ministers and their staff'.
74 For a summary account of public service reform in the 1980s, see this author's 'Prime ministers and their staff', pp.39–43.
75 Carroll and Manne's essays in their *Shutdown*, for instance.
76 Anthony Giddens, *Modernity and Self-Identity*, p.27.
77 Terry Eagleton, *Ideology: An introduction*, Verso, London, 1991, p.40.

Chapter 6   Constructive alternatives

1   James Walter, 'Ideas fill the political vacuum', *Australian* Higher Education Supplement, 23 February 1994.
2   Wolfgang Kasper *et al.*, *Australia at the Crossroads: Our choices to the year 2000*, Harcourt Brace Jovanovich, Sydney, 1980.
3   Wolfgang Kasper, 'Death of the political idea', Letters to the editor, *Australian*, 2 March 1994. All subsequent quotations in this paragraph are from this letter.
4   Hugo Hinsley, 'Docklands is not the only future', in Walter, Spearritt & Hinsley, eds, *Changing Cities*.
5   NG Butlin, A Barnard and JJ Pincus, *Government and Capitalism*, Allen & Unwin, Sydney, 1982.
6   Tom Fitzgerald, 'Japan in fact and theory', in his *Between Life and Economics: 1990 Boyer Lectures* (second edition), Australian Broadcasting Corporation, Sydney, 1991, pp.25–36.
7   Anatole Kaletsky, 'Keynes country', *Australian*, 13 July 1993.
8   Geoff Dow, 'The economic consequences of economists', *Australian Journal of Political Science*, vol.27, no.2, 1992, pp.265–66.
9   Dow, 'The economic consequences of economists', p.269.
10 Dow, 'The economic consequences of economists', pp.269–73.
11 Dow, 'The economic consequences of economists', p.271.
12 Brian Dollery, 'The economic consequences of economists: comment', *Australian Journal of Political Science*, vol.28, no.1, 1993, pp.146–49. And see, too, Dow's acerbic response in the same issue, pp.150–52.
13 John Langmore and John Quiggin, *Work for All: Full employment in the nineties*, Melbourne University Press, Melbourne, 1994.
14 See, for instance, William Keegan, *The Spectre of Capitalism: The Future of the World Economy After the Fall of Communism*, Radius, London, 1992.
15 Dow, 'The economic consequences of economists', pp.262–63.
16 Dow, 'The economic consequences of economists', pp.263–65.
17 Keegan, *The Spectre of Capitalism*.
18 Keegan, *The Spectre of Capitalism*, p.92.
19 J Langmore and T Quiggin, *Work for All*, pp.143–44; and see chapter 8 in its entirety.
20 Langmore & Quiggin, *Work for All*, pp.119–21.
21 Paul Krugman, 'A dangerous obsession', *Australian*, 28 March 1994.

22 Krugman, 'A dangerous obsession'.
23 Emy, *Remaking Australia*.
24 Emy, *Remaking Australia*, p.183.
25 Emy, *Remaking Australia*, pp.182–89.
26 Emy, *Remaking Australia*, pp. 191, 192, 195.
27 Emy, *Remaking Australia*, chapter 8.
28 Emy, *Remaking Australia*, p.201.
29 Emy, *Remaking Australia*, p.202.
30 Stephen Bell, 'Weak on the state: economic rationalism in Canberra', *Australian and New Zealand Journal of Sociology*, vol. 29, no. 3, November 1993, p.398.
31 Mike Davis, *City of Quartz*, Verso, London, 1990.
32 See Brian Head and Elaine McCoy, eds, *Deregulation or Better Regulation*, Macmillan, Melbourne, 1991.
33 On the media monoculture, see Graeme Turner, *Making It National: Nationalism and Australian popular culture*, Allen & Unwin, Sydney, 1994, especially chapters 2 and 7.

Chapter 7   Reviving political imagination

1 This argument was first mooted by TH Marshall, *Citizenship and Social Class and Other Essays*, Cambridge University Press, Cambridge, 1950.
2 See Chilla Bulbeck, 'Citizenship' in her *Social Sciences in Australia: An introduction*, Harcourt Brace Jovanovich, Sydney, 1993, pp.205–46.
3 See, for instance, Michael Mann, 'Ruling class strategies and citizenship', *Sociology*, vol.21, no.3, 1987, pp.339–54; U Vogel, 'Is citizenship gender-specific?' in U Vogel and M Moran, eds, *The Frontiers of Citizenship*, Macmillan, London 1991; MA Quinn, *Immigration, Ethnicity and Citizenship in Australia, France and Germany: A revision of Marshall's thesis*, BA Honours Thesis, Faculty of Humanities, Griffith University, Brisbane, 1993.
4 Harvey, *The Condition of Postmodernity*, ibid pp.66–98; Davis, *City of Quartz*, ibid pp.223–63.
5 Patricia Hewitt, *'Fellow Australian: Citizenship, sex and power'*, The Third Donald Horne Address, National Centre for Australian Studies, Melbourne, 1994, p.5; H Arendt, *The Human Condition*, Doubleday Anchor, New York, 1959, chapter 2.
6 Anne Phillips, quoted in Hewitt, *'Fellow Australian . . .'*, p.5.
7 This is to extend Alastair Davidson's argument in his *Invisible State: The formation of the Australian state 1788–1901*, Cambridge University Press, Sydney, 1991.
8 This is the argument made by Nancy Viviani in her 'Reinventing the wheel of Australian citizenship', paper given at the Bureau of Immigration Research Outlook Conference, Melbourne, December 1992.

9 Bauer, quoted in Viviani, 'Reinventing the wheel of Australian citizenship'.

10 Antony Black, 'Civil Society' in David Miller, ed., *The Blackwell Encyclopaedia of Political Thought*, Blackwell, Oxford, 1991, p.77.

11 See, for instance, 'Right-wing institute rethinks doctrine', *The Independent* (UK), 27 September 1993; 'Thatcherism fails test', *The Guardian Weekly*, 3 October 1993—both reporting on the conservative response to David Green, *Reinventing Civil Society: The rediscovery of welfare without politics*, The Institute of Economic Affairs, London, 1993.

12 Michael Walzer, 'The Civil Society Argument', in Chantal Mouffe, ed., *Dimensions of Radical Democracy*, Routledge, London, 1992, p.95; Jean L Cohen and Andrew Arato, *Civil Society and Political Theory*, The MIT Press, Cambridge, Mass., 1992, p.24.

13 Charles Taylor, 'Modes of civil society', *Public Culture*, vol.3, no.1, Fall 1990, p.111.

14 This is one reading of Davidson's *The Invisible State* (though not the one Davidson would prefer).

15 Manning Clark, for instance (see his *A History of Australia, Volume 5*, chapters 5 and 6). Paul Keating was a prominent exponent of this view.

16 See Davidson, *The Invisible State*, for instance.

17 CS Blackton, 'Australian nationality and nationalism, 1850–1900', *Historical Studies*, vol.9, no.36, 1961, pp.351–67.

18 Helen Irving, 'Who were the republicans?' in D Headon, J Warden and B Gammage, eds, *Crown or Country: The traditions of Australian republicanism*, Allen & Unwin, Sydney, 1994, p.78.

19 The best essay on this is Marshall Berman's, *All That Is Solid Melts Into Air: The experience of modernity*, Verso, London, 1983, pp.87–129.

20 Cohen and Arato, *Civil Society and Political Theory*, p.25.

21 Kai Nielsen, 'Reconceptualising civil society for now', *Arena Journal*, no.2, 1993–94, p.173.

22 See, for instance, F Stevens, ed., *Racism: The Australian experience*, ANZ Book Co., Brookvale, 1971; Andrew Markus, *Fear and Hatred: Purifying Australia and California 1850–1901*, Hale & Iremonger, Sydney, 1979; Marilyn Lake, 'The politics of respectability: identifying the masculinist context', *Historical Studies*, vol.22, no.86, 1986, pp.116–31.

23 Irving, 'Who were the republicans?', p.78.

24 Anthony D Smith, 'The origins of nations', *Ethnic and Racial Studies*, vol.12, no.3, 1989, p.342.

25 For the principal touchstones, see Anderson, *Imagined Communities*; Ernest Gellner, *Nations and Nationalism*, Blackwell, Oxford, 1983; EJ Hobsbawm, *Nations and Nationalism since 1780*, Cambridge University Press, Cambridge, 1990; Anthony D Smith, *National Identity*, Penguin, London, 1991.

26 Turner, *Making It National*.

27 George Orwell, 'Notes on nationalism' in his *Decline of the English Murder and other essays*, Penguin, Harmondsworth, 1965, pp.155–79.

28 Stephen Castles, Mary Kalantzis, Bill Cope and Michael Morrissey, *Mistaken Identity: Multiculturalism and the demise of nationalism in Australia*, Pluto Press, Sydney, 1988, p.139.

29 Patricia Grimshaw, Marilyn Lake, Ann McGrath & Marian Quartly, *Creating a Nation 1788–1990*, McPhee Gribble, Ringwood, 1994.

30 Grimshaw *et al.*, *Creating a Nation*, p.2.

31 Grimshaw *et al.*, *Creating a Nation*, p.314.

32 Turner, *Making It National*, pp.158–9.

33 Turner, *Making It National*, p.157.

34 Turner, *Making It National*, p.159.

35 This point is strongly made by Docker in his *The Nervous Nineties*; and in *Dilemmas of Identity*.

36 Stuart Macintyre, *The Oxford History of Australia, Volume 4 1901–1942: The succeeding age*, Oxford University Press, Melbourne, p.x.

37 W Stephenson, *The play theory of mass communication*, University of Chicago Press, Chicago, 1967, p.93.

38 Eduardo Galeano, 'Celebration of contradictions', in *The Book of Embraces*, Norton, New York, 1991, p.125.

39 Crick, *In Defence of Politics*, p.121.

40 See, for instance, Docker, *The Nervous Nineties*.

41 Though see John Hirst's retort to this point, 'Can subjects be citizens?' in Headon *et al.*, *Crown or Country*, pp.118–23.

42 AA Phillips, 'The cultural cringe' in his *The Australian Tradition*, Longman Cheshire, Melbourne, 1966, p.116.

43 Giddens, *Modernity and Self-Identity*, p.27.

44 See, for instance, Headon *et al.*, *Crown or Country*; Brian Galligan, 'Regularising the Australian Republic', *AJPS*, vol.28, 1993, pp.56–66; John Uhr, 'Instituting republicanism: parliamentary vices, republican virtues?', *AJPS*, vol.28, 1993, pp.27–39; Philip Pettit, 'Our republican heritage', ABC Radio National, 1 March 1994.

45 Uhr, 'Instituting republicanism . . .', p.31.

46 Pettit, 'Our republican heritage', text p.2.

47 For an overview of this position, see Alastair Davidson, '*Res publica* and citizen' in Headon *et al.*, *Crown or Country*, pp.170–72.

48 For much more extensive discussion of such an argument, see David Harvey, 'Social justice, postmodernism and the city', in Walter, Spearritt and Hinsley, eds, *Changing Cities*, pp.19–41.

49 See Anna Yeatman, 'Voice and representation in the politics of difference' in Sneja Gunew and Anna Yeatman, eds, *Feminism and the Politics of Difference*, Allen & Unwin, Sydney, 1993, pp.228–45.

50 See, for instance, the continuing debate in *Arena Magazine* involving Helen Irving (no.8, Dec–Jan. 1993–94, pp.24–26), Ann Curthoys (no.8, pp.27–28), Marilyn Lake (no.9, Feb–Mar 1994, pp.32–33), Cheryl Kernot (no.10, April–May 1994, pp.25–26) and letters from Chilla

Bulbeck, Helen Irving and Alan Atkinson (no.11, June–July 1994, pp.14–16).

51 Yeatman, 'Voice and representation in the politics of difference', p.228.

52 Marilyn Lake, 'A republic for women?' *Arena Magazine*, no.9, Feb–Mar 1994, p.32.

53 John Braithwaite and Philip Pettit, *Not Just Deserts: A republican conception of criminal justice*, Oxford University Press, Oxford, 1990; Philip Pettit, 'Liberalism and republicanism', *Australian Journal of Political Science*, vol.28, Special Issue, 1993, pp.162–89.

54 Pettit, 'Liberalism and republicanism', p.173.

55 Pettit, 'Liberalism and republicanism', p.180.

56 See James Walter, 'Intellectuals and the political culture' in B Head and J Walter, eds, *Intellectual Movements and Australian Society*, Oxford University Press, Melbourne, 1988; and James Walter, 'Intellectuals', in R Nile, ed., *Australian Civilization*, Oxford University Press, Melbourne, 1994.

57 This is more extensively argued in Walter, 'Intellectuals and political culture'.

58 See Ian Lowe, *Our Universities Are Turning Us Into the 'Ignorant Country'*, University of New South Wales Press, Sydney, 1994.

59 Pusey, *Economic Rationalism in Canberra*.

60 See LF Crisp, *Ben Chifley: A biography*, Longman, London, 1955; Walter, *The Leader*; Weller, *Malcolm Fraser PM*.

61 See Turner, *Making It National*.

62 David Bowman, *The Captive Press*, Penguin, Ringwood, 1988.

Index

The Future of Capitalism
How today's economic forces will shape tomorrow's world
Lester Thurow

This is a time of great economic change. Irrepressible forces are playing off each other and radically altering our world—the breakdown of the communist world, the rise of technology industries, changing demographics, a truly global economy, and the lack of a dominant economic, political, or military world leader. Lester Thurow, one of America's most influential and popular economists, sets your mind alight with his sweep of the forces of today and the possibilities of tomorrow. Capitalism and all its players must respond to these forces, and *The Future of Capitalism* charts the attitudes and actions we need.

November 1975
Paul Kelly

The sacking of the Whitlam government on 11 November 1975 remains the greatest crisis in Australia's political history. Leading political analyst and author Paul Kelly revisits that tumultuous time to provide a new insight into what really happened in the months, weeks and days leading up to the Dismissal.

He looks at the personalities of the key players, the manoeuvring behind the scenes, the tricks to control the Senate, the battles to establish the moral high ground and the failed compromises. Interviews with many of the protagonists shed new light on the complex chain of events that began with the election of the Whitlam government in 1972 and led to its dismissal three years later.

This is a story of high drama, of towering egos and political intrigue that changed the face of Australian politics forever.

The matchless grasp of Australian politics demonstrated in Paul Kelly's classic *The End of Certainty* has led to a book that is essential reading for a whole new generation of Australians, as well as all those who can remember the drama of the Dismissal.

Rooting Democracy
Growing the society we want
Moira Rayner

Parliament alone is unable to protect the public interest while safeguarding individual rights, argues Moira Rayner. For a flourishing democracy with properly accountable government, we must protect and develop those less visible—and thus more vulnerable—institutions, such as public prosecutors, commissioners for human rights, the independence of the public service, FOI, ombudsmen, and other 'watchdogs' that provide the checks and balances vital to democracy. Polemical yet reflective, Rayner's lively and far-sighted analysis makes essential reading for students and teachers of civics—indeed for all who value a truly participatory democracy and civil society.

Power and Prospects
Reflections on human nature and the social order
Noam Chomsky

Noam Chomsky has been described as 'the world's greatest dissident' and 'arguably the most important intellectual alive'. For 30 years, his views have alerted an increasingly concerned public to the true nature of power. His perceptive descriptions of how the public is excluded from decision-making and policy formation provide new insights to major events in the world today.

From East Timor to the Middle East, from the nature of democracy to our place in the natural world, from the intellectual responsibility of writers to anarchic visions, from international politics to the politics of language, *Power and Prospects* provides a scathing critique of orthodox views and government policy. Chomsky lifts a veil of lies diverting the public from knowledge of the heinous acts being committed in their name. He reveals how the 'new' world order is remarketing the same old disorder. His refreshingly clear views of the world and the nature of things are supported by a wealth of detail.

The works contained in *Power and Prospects* reflect Chomsky's latest thinking on a broad range of themes. The book is based upon a series of addresses he delivered to sell-out audiences on his 1995 visit to Australia.

Unlocking the Infrastructure
The reform of public utilities in Australia
Rodney Maddock and Stephen King

The nation's infrastructure is undergoing the most intensive microeconomic, legal and political reform of its history as the recommendations of the Hilmer Report are implemented. However, the anticipated benefits of these reforms depend on a range of assumptions and ideologies concerning the best design of public and private infrastructure. This book examines those assumptions, the reforms themselves, and how the vision of the reforms may work in practice.

Issues explored include the public utility problem, pricing, natural monopolies, access to essential infrastructure, investment incentives and integration of services. All industries are covered, with extensive case studies of telecommunications, rail and gas being provided.

The Paradox of Parties
Australian political parties in the 1990s
Edited by Marian Simms

Is the Australian political system in crisis? *The Paradox of Parties* argues that despite the many claims that our party system is overloaded and in crisis, it is actually remarkably durable.

The Paradox of Parties examines how well the three major parties, the ALP, the Liberals and the Nationals, have adapted to economic and social changes. The results are mixed. For the ALP and the Liberals in particular, declining and ageing memberships have been a problem. Like the rest of Australian political culture, all three parties are masculinist in nature and the ALP's attempts to provide a structural solution have been unsuccessful. Yet these parties still dominate Australian politics and are likely to do so in the future.

With contributions from leading political practitioners and local and international political commentators, *The Paradox of Parties* is essential reading for anyone interested in Australian politics today.